Reading Mastery

CLASSIC EDITION

Spelling Book

Level II

Siegfried Engelmann
Elaine C. Bruner

A Division of The McGraw·Hill Companies

Columbus, Ohio

www.sra4kids.com

SRA/McGraw-Hill

A Division of The McGraw-Hill Companies

Send all inquiries to:
SRA/McGraw-Hill
8787 Orion Place
Columbus, OH 43240-4027

Printed in the United States of America.

ISBN 0-07-569324-0

3 4 5 6 7 8 9 IPC 06 05 04

Introduction

There are 79 lessons in the Reading Mastery Classic Edition, Level II spelling program. In these 79 lessons, and in the first 79 lessons of the reading program, the children spell by sounds rather than by letter names.

At lesson 83 in the reading program, the children are introduced to all the letter names and begin the transition from spelling by sounds to spelling by letter names. By lesson 85, they are ready to begin a spelling program that is independent of the reading program.*

Materials Needed

The materials required for the spelling program are this spelling book, which contains detailed directions for presenting each lesson; lined paper and pencils for the children to use; and a chalkboard for presenting some of the tasks.

Placement

The children can enter the spelling program at one of two lessons—1 or 11. Children who are placed at lesson 11 in the reading program begin at lesson 11 in the spelling program.

Scheduling

The amount of time required for each spelling lesson is approximately ten minutes. The spelling lessons should not be presented as a part of the reading lesson, but can be scheduled at any other time during the day.

The spelling program can be presented to either the entire class or to small groups. Note that, if the program is presented to the entire class, you begin with lesson 1 (unless all of the children in the class are scheduled to begin the reading program at lesson 11).

*The authors recommend SRA's direct-instruction spelling program, *Spelling Mastery, Level A.*

Skipping Lessons

If the children in a group skip reading lessons on the basis of performance, they can skip the corresponding spelling lessons. In other words, if the children skip reading lesson 38, they can also skip spelling lesson 38. In this way, you will be working with the same spelling lesson and reading lesson each day with a given group. For more information on skipping reading lessons, see the Teacher's Guide.

General Procedures

Give each child lined paper and a pencil. It is preferable for the children to write the dictated sounds in lessons 1–35 in a row (across) instead of a column (down the paper). The children should write dictated words in a column.

Overview of Skills Taught
Spelling by sounds

Lessons 1 through 10 consist of a review of words that were presented in the Level I spelling program. During these lessons, the children write sounds from dictation. The children also write words after they say the sounds in the word "the hard way," which means with pauses between the sounds.

Beginning with lesson 11, the children write sound combinations from dictation. The first sound combinations introduced are **ar** and **th.** Other combinations introduced in the program are **sh, ing, al, wh, er,** and **ck.**

Beginning at lesson 12, the children write words that contain the sound combination **th** (introduced in lesson 11). The teacher writes words containing the sound combination **th** on the board. The children first read these words and say the sounds for each of the words. After the teacher erases the board, the children write the words.

After the children have worked with a given sound combination for four lessons, they are introduced to an abbreviated format in which they say the sounds for a word and then write the word. (This format begins in lesson 14 with **th** words.)

Beginning at lesson 21, irregular words are introduced in the spelling program. In the introductory format, the teacher presents a variation of the irregular format used in reading: "When you write the word **was,** you write these sounds: **www aaa sss.**" The children say the sounds. Then they write the word.

After an irregular word has appeared in the introductory format for one or two lessons, it appears in an abbreviated format in which the children say the sounds for the word (without a teacher demonstration) and then write the word.

In lesson 15, the children are introduced to a review format. The words that appear in this format are words that have appeared frequently in the preceding lessons, or are new, easy, regular words. This format does not call for the children to say the sounds in a word before writing it. The children are instructed to "think about the sounds in _____ and write the word."

Sentence writing is introduced in lesson 21. The children write one sentence during each lesson until lesson 36, at which time two sentences are introduced in each lesson.

The words used in sentence writing have been presented frequently and must have appeared in the review format. The teacher says the sentence the children are to write. The children repeat the sentence. Then they say it the slow way (with a pause between the words). After that, they write the sentence.

Important information

1. The spelling program does not rely on joined letters or macrons (long lines over long vowels). Children are not to write either joined letters or macrons. Children also do not write capital letters.

2. If an **e** appears on the end of a word, call the sound **ēēē** when sounding out the word (not **eee** as in **end**). Spelling by letter names comes easier to the children if they are used to referring to the **e**'s on the end of words by the letter name.

3. If a vowel in a word is long (the name of a vowel letter), say the long vowel sound when sounding out the word.

Examples:

The **o** in **over** would be **ōōō** (since it is pronounced long in the word).

The first **e** in **ever** would be **eee** (since it is not pronounced long in the word).

The **o** in **not** would be short: **ooo.**

The **o** in **no** would be long: **ōōō.**

General Correction Procedures

If the children make mistakes, follow the correction procedure of (1) model and (2) test.

If you ask the children to say the sounds in the word **man,** and they make mistakes:

1. (Model) **Here are the sounds in man. Listen. mmm** (pause) **aaa** (pause) **nnn.**

2. (Test) **Your turn. Say the sounds in man.** Clap for each sound as children say *mmm* (pause) *aaa* (pause) *nnn.*

If a child makes a mistake when you ask the children to think about the sounds in the word **stop** and write the word:

1. (Model) **Here are the sounds in the word stop. Listen. sss** (pause) **t** (pause) **ooo** (pause) **p.**

2. (Test) **Your turn. Say the sounds in stop.** Clap for each sound as the children say *sss* (pause) *t* (pause) *ooo* (pause) *p.*

3. (Delayed test) **Think about the sounds in stop and write the word.** Check work.

Summary of Skills Taught

At the end of the spelling program, the children can spell regular words and some irregular words by sounds, and they can write the words accurately. They can spell by sounds words that contain common sound combinations, such as **ar, al, sh, th,** and **wh.** They can accurately spell the words in a variety of simple sentence forms, including questions and some fairly long statements.

LESSON 1

SOUND WRITING

TASK 1   Write **h, s, a, r, e, t**

a. You're going to write some sounds.
b. Here's the first sound you're going to write. Listen. **h**. What sound? (Signal.) *h*.
c. Write **h**. Check work.
d. Next sound. Listen. **sss**. What sound? (Signal.) *sss*.
e. Write **sss**. Check work.
f. Repeat *d* and *e* for **a, r, e,** and **t**.

WORD WRITING

TASK 2   Read, say the sounds, write **rat**

a. Write **rat** on the board.
b. Everybody, read this word the fast way. Get ready. (Signal.) *Rat*. What word? (Signal.) *Rat*. Yes, **rat**.
c. My turn to say the sounds in **rat** the hard way. Touch each sound. **Rrr** (pause) **aaa** (pause) **t**.
d. Your turn. Say the sounds in **rat** the hard way. Get ready. Touch each sound as children say *rrr* (pause) *aaa* (pause) *t*.
e. Erase **rat**. I'll clap for each sound. You say the sounds in **rat** the hard way. Get ready. Clap for each sound as children say *rrr* (pause) *aaa* (pause) *t*. Repeat until firm.
f. Everybody, write the word (pause) **rat**. Check work.

TASK 3   Read, say the sounds, write **sat**

a. Write **sat** on the board.
b. Everybody, read this word the fast way. Get ready. (Signal.) *Sat*. What word? (Signal.) *Sat*. Yes, **sat**.
c. My turn to say the sounds in **sat** the hard way. Touch each sound. **Sss** (pause) **aaa** (pause) **t**.
d. Your turn. Say the sounds in **sat** the hard way. Get ready. Touch each sound as children say *sss* (pause) *aaa* (pause) *t*.
e. Erase **sat**. I'll clap for each sound. You say the sounds in **sat** the hard way. Get ready. Clap for each sound as children say *sss* (pause) *aaa* (pause) *t*. Repeat until firm.
f. Everybody, write the word (pause) **sat**. Check work.

TASK 4   Read, say the sounds, write **hat**

a. Write **hat** on the board.
b. Everybody, read this word the fast way. Get ready. (Signal.) *Hat*. What word? (Signal.) *Hat*. Yes, **hat**.
c. My turn to say the sounds in **hat** the hard way. Touch each sound. **H** (pause) **aaa** (pause) **t**.
d. Your turn. Say the sounds in **hat** the hard way. Get ready. Touch each sound as children say *h* (pause) *aaa* (pause) *t*.
e. Erase **hat**. I'll clap for each sound. You say the sounds in **hat** the hard way. Get ready. Clap for each sound as children say *h* (pause) *aaa* (pause) *t*. Repeat until firm.
f. Everybody, write the word (pause) **hat**. Check work.

TASK 5   Read, say the sounds, write **he**

a. Write **he** on the board.
b. Everybody, read this word the fast way. Get ready. (Signal.) *He*. What word? (Signal.) *He*. Yes, **he**.
c. My turn to say the sounds in **he** the hard way. Touch each sound. **H** (pause) $\overline{eee}$.
d. Your turn. Say the sounds in **he** the hard way. Get ready. Touch each sound as children say *h* (pause) $\overline{eee}$.
e. Erase **he**. I'll clap for each sound. You say the sounds in **he** the hard way. Get ready. Clap for each sound as children say *h* (pause) $\overline{eee}$. Repeat until firm.
f. Everybody, write the word (pause) **he**. Check work.

LESSON 2

SOUND WRITING

TASK 1   Write **h, s, r, a, e, t**

a. You're going to write some sounds.
b. Here's the first sound you're going to write. Listen. **h**. What sound? (Signal.) *h*.
c. Write **h**. Check work.
d. Next sound. Listen. **sss**. What sound? (Signal.) *sss*.
e. Write **sss**. Check work.
f. Repeat *d* and *e* for **r, a, e,** and **t**.

WORD WRITING

TASK 2   Read, say the sounds, write **he**, **hat**, **sat**

a. Write **he** on the board.
b. Everybody, read this word the fast way. Get ready.   (Signal.) *He*. What word? (Signal.) *He*. Yes, **he**.
c. My turn to say the sounds in **he** the hard way.   Touch each sound. H (pause) ēēē.
d. Your turn. Say the sounds in **he** the hard way. Get ready.   Touch each sound as children say *h* (pause) ēēē.
e. Erase **he**. I'll clap for each sound. You say the sounds in **he** the hard way. Get ready. Clap for each sound as children say *h* (pause) ēēē. Repeat until firm.
f. Everybody, write the word   (pause) **he**. Check work.
g. Repeat *a* through *f* for **hat** and **sat**.

TASK 3   Read, say the sounds, write **rat**

a. Write **rat** on the board.
b. Everybody, read this word the fast way. Get ready.   (Signal.) *Rat*. What word? (Signal.) *Rat*. Yes, **rat**.
c. Say the sounds in **rat** the hard way. Touch each sound as the children say *rrr* (pause) *aaa* (pause) *t*.
d. Erase **rat**. I'll clap for each sound. You say the sounds in **rat** the hard way. Get ready.   Clap for each sound as the children say *rrr* (pause) *aaa* (pause) *t*. Repeat until firm.
e. Everybody, write the word   (pause) **rat**. Check work.

LESSON 3

SOUND WRITING

TASK 1   Write **a**, **h**, **m**, **e**, **t**, **s**

a. You're going to write some sounds.
b. Here's the first sound you're going to write. Listen. **aaa**. What sound?   (Signal.) *aaa*.
c. Write **aaa**.   Check work.
d. Next sound. Listen. **h**. What sound? (Signal.) *h*.
e. Write **h**.   Check work.
f. Repeat *d* and *e* for **m**, **e**, **t**, and **s**.

WORD WRITING

TASK 2   Read, say the sounds, write **me**, **mat**

a. Write **me** on the board.
b. Everybody, read this word the fast way. Get ready.   (Signal.) *Me*. What word? (Signal.) *Me*. Yes, **me**.
c. My turn to say the sounds in **me** the hard way.   Touch each sound. Mmm (pause) ēēē.
d. Your turn. Say the sounds in **me** the hard way. Get ready.   Touch each sound as children say *mmm* (pause) ēēē.
e. Erase **me**. I'll clap for each sound. You say the sounds in **me** the hard way. Get ready. Clap for each sound as children say *mmm* (pause) ēēē. Repeat until firm.
f. Everybody, write the word   (pause) **me**. Check work.
g. Repeat *a* through *f* for **mat**.

TASK 3   Read, say the sounds, write **sam**, **sat**

Children are not responsible for capital letters.

a. Write **sam** on the board.
b. Everybody, read this word the fast way. Get ready.   (Signal.) *Sam*. What word? (Signal.) *Sam*. Yes, **Sam**.
c. Say the sounds in **Sam** the hard way. Touch each sound as the children say *Sss* (pause) *aaa* (pause) *mmm*.
d. Erase **sam**. I'll clap for each sound. You say the sounds in **Sam** the hard way. Get ready.   Clap for each sound as the children say *Sss* (pause) *aaa* (pause) *mmm*. Repeat until firm.
e. Everybody, write the word   (pause) **Sam**. Check work.
f. Repeat *a* through *e* for **sat**.

LESSON 4

SOUND WRITING

TASK 1   Write **m**, **r**, **n**, **a**, **t**, **e**

a. You're going to write some sounds.
b. Here's the first sound you're going to write. Listen. **mmm**. What sound?   (Signal.) *mmm*.
c. Write **mmm**.   Check work.
d. Next sound. Listen. **rrr**. What sound? (Signal.) *rrr*.
e. Write **rrr**.   Check work.
f. Repeat *d* and *e* for **n**, **a**, **t**, and **e**.

WORD WRITING

TASK 2   Read, say the sounds, write **ram**

a. Write **ram** on the board.
b. Everybody, read this word the fast way. Get ready. (Signal.) *Ram.* What word? (Signal.) *Ram.* Yes, **ram**.
c. My turn to say the sounds in **ram** the hard way. Touch each sound. **Rrr** (pause) **aaa** (pause) **mmm**.
d. Your turn. Say the sounds in **ram** the hard way. Get ready. Touch each sound as children say *rrr* (pause) *aaa* (pause) *mmm*.
e. Erase **ram**. I'll clap for each sound. You say the sounds in **ram** the hard way. Get ready. Clap for each sound as children say *rrr* (pause) *aaa* (pause) *mmm*. Repeat until firm.
f. Everybody, write the word (pause) **ram**. Check work.

TASK 3   Read, say the sounds, write **sam**, **mat**

a. Write **sam** on the board.
b. Everybody, read this word the fast way. Get ready. (Signal.) *Sam.* What word? (Signal.) *Sam.* Yes, **Sam**.
c. Say the sounds in **Sam** the hard way. Touch each sound as the children say *Sss* (pause) *aaa* (pause) *mmm*.
d. Erase **sam**. I'll clap for each sound. You say the sounds in **Sam** the hard way. Get ready. Clap for each sound as the children say *Sss* (pause) *aaa* (pause) *mmm*. Repeat until firm.
e. Everybody, write the word (pause) **Sam**. Check work.
f. Repeat *a* through *e* for **mat**.

TASK 4   Say the sounds, write **me**

a. You're going to write the word (pause) **me**. Say the sounds in **me**. Get ready. Clap for each sound as the children say *mmm* (pause) *ēēē*. Repeat until firm.
b. Everybody, write the word (pause) **me**. Check work.

TASK 5   Listen, say the sounds, write **see**

a. You're going to write the word (pause) **see**. When you write the word **see**, you write these sounds: *sss* (pause) *ēēē* (pause) *ēēē*.
b. Say the sounds you write for (pause) **see**. Get ready. Clap for each sound as the children say *sss* (pause) *ēēē* (pause) *ēēē*. Repeat until firm.
c. Everybody, write the word (pause) **see**. Check work.

LESSON 5

SOUND WRITING

TASK 1   Write **f, t, h, r, m, e, s**

a. You're going to write some sounds.
b. Here's the first sound you're going to write. Listen. **fff**. What sound? (Signal.) *fff*.
c. Write **fff**. Check work.
d. Next sound. Listen. **t**. What sound? (Signal.) *t*.
e. Write **t**. Check work.
f. Repeat *d* and *e* for **h, r, m, e**, and **s**.

WORD WRITING

TASK 2   Read, say the sounds, write **see**, **at, am**

a. Write **see** on the board.
b. Everybody, read this word the fast way. Get ready. (Signal.) *See.* What word? (Signal.) *See.* Yes, **see**.
c. Say the sounds in **see** the hard way. Touch each sound as the children say *sss* (pause) *ēēē* (pause) *ēēē*.
d. Erase **see**. I'll clap for each sound. You say the sounds in **see** the hard way. Get ready. Clap for each sound as the children say *sss* (pause) *ēēē* (pause) *ēēē*. Repeat until firm.
e. Everybody, write the word (pause) **see**. Check work.
f. Repeat *a* through *e* for **at** and **am**.

TASK 3   Say the sounds, write **ram**, **ham**

a. You're going to write the word (pause) **ram**. Say the sounds in **ram**. Get ready. Clap for each sound as the children say *rrr* (pause) *aaa* (pause) *mmm*. Repeat until firm.
b. Everybody, write the word (pause) **ram**. Check work.
c. Repeat *a* and *b* for **ham**.

LESSON 6

SOUND WRITING

TASK 1   Write a, f, r, t, h, e

a. You're going to write some sounds.
b. Here's the first sound you're going to write. Listen. **aaa**. What sound? (Signal.) *aaa*.
c. Write **aaa**. Check work.
d. Next sound. Listen. **fff**. What sound? (Signal.) *fff*.
e. Write **fff**. Check work.
f. Repeat *d* and *e* for **r, t, h,** and **e**.

WORD WRITING

TASK 2   Read, say the sounds, write see, fat

a. Write **see** on the board.
b. Everybody, read this word the fast way. Get ready. (Signal.) *See*. What word? (Signal.) *See*. Yes, **see**.
c. Say the sounds in **see** the hard way. Touch each sound as the children say *sss* (pause) *ēēē* (pause) *ēēē*.
d. Erase **see**. I'll clap for each sound. You say the sounds in **see** the hard way. Get ready. Clap for each sound as the children say *sss* (pause) *ēēē* (pause) *ēēē*. Repeat until firm.
e. Everybody, write the word (pause) **see**. Check work.
f. Repeat *a* through *e* for **fat**.

TASK 3   Say the sounds, write am, ham, ram

a. You're going to write the word (pause) **am**. Say the sounds in **am**. Get ready. Clap for each sound as the children say *aaa* (pause) *mmm*. Repeat until firm.
b. Everybody, write the word (pause) **am**. Check work.
c. Repeat *a* and *b* for **ham** and **ram**.

LESSON 7

SOUND WRITING

TASK 1   Write h, r, a, f, t, e, s

a. You're going to write some sounds.
b. Here's the first sound you're going to write. Listen. **h**. What sound? (Signal.) *h*.
c. Write **h**. Check work.
d. Next sound. Listen. **rrr**. What sound? (Signal.) *rrr*.
e. Write **rrr**. Check work.
f. Repeat *d* and *e* for **a, f, t, e,** and **s**.

WORD WRITING

TASK 2   Say the sounds, write he, me, see, mat, am, at

a. You're going to write the word (pause) **he**. Say the sounds in **he**. Get ready. Clap for each sound as the children say *h* (pause) *ēēē*. Repeat until firm.
b. Everybody, write the word (pause) **he**. Check work.
c. Repeat *a* and *b* for **me, see, mat, am,** and **at**.

LESSON 8

SOUND WRITING

TASK 1   Write i, a, e, f, m, h, t

a. You're going to write some sounds.
b. Here's the first sound you're going to write. Listen. **iii**. What sound? (Signal.) *iii*.
c. Write **iii**. Check work.
d. Next sound. Listen. **aaa**. What sound? (Signal.) *aaa*.
e. Write **aaa**. Check work.
f. Repeat *d* and *e* for **e, f, m, h,** and **t**.

WORD WRITING

TASK 2   Say the sounds, write me, am, ram, at, sat, fat

a. You're going to write the word (pause) **me**. Say the sounds in **me**. Get ready. Clap for each sound as the children say *mmm* (pause) *ēēē*. Repeat until firm.
b. Everybody, write the word (pause) **me**. Check work.
c. Repeat *a* and *b* for **am, ram, at, sat,** and **fat**.

LESSON 9

SOUND WRITING

TASK 1 Write i, f, e, s, a, h

a. You're going to write some sounds.
b. Here's the first sound you're going to write. Listen. **iii**. What sound? (Signal.) *iii*.
c. Write **iii**. Check work.
d. Next sound. Listen. **fff**. What sound? (Signal.) *fff*.
e. Write **fff**. Check work.
f. Repeat *d* and *e* for **e, s, a,** and **h**.

WORD WRITING

TASK 2 Read, say the sounds, write it, fit

a. Write **it** on the board.
b. Everybody, read this word the fast way. Get ready. (Signal.) *It*. What word? (Signal.) *It*. Yes, **it**.
c. Say the sounds in **it** the hard way. Touch each sound as the children say *iii* (pause) *t*.
d. Erase **it**. I'll clap for each sound. You say the sounds in **it** the hard way. Get ready. Clap for each sound as the children say *iii* (pause) *t*. Repeat until firm.
e. Everybody, write the word (pause) **it**.
f. Repeat *a* through *e* for **fit**.

TASK 3 Say the sounds, write ham, at, hat, fat

a. You're going to write the word (pause) **ham**. Say the sounds in **ham**. Get ready. Clap for each sound as the children say *h* (pause) *aaa* (pause) *mmm*. Repeat until firm.
b. Everybody, write the word (pause) **ham**.
c. Repeat *a* and *b* for **at, hat,** and **fat**.

LESSON 10

SOUND WRITING

TASK 1 Write i, e, a, t, s, m, f

a. You're going to write some sounds.
b. Here's the first sound you're going to write. Listen. **iii**. What sound? (Signal.) *iii*.
c. Write **iii**. Check work.
d. Next sound. Listen. **eee**. What sound? (Signal.) *eee*.
e. Write **eee**. Check work.
f. Repeat *d* and *e* for **a, t, s, m,** and **f**.

WORD WRITING

TASK 2 Read, say the sounds, write if, it

a. Write **if** on the board.
b. Everybody, read this word the fast way. Get ready. (Signal.) *If*. What word? (Signal.) *If*. Yes, **if**.
c. Say the sounds in **if** the hard way. Touch each sound as the children say *iii* (pause) *fff*.
d. Erase **if**. I'll clap for each sound. You say the sounds in **if** the hard way. Get ready. Clap for each sound as the children say *iii* (pause) *fff*. Repeat until firm.
e. Everybody, write the word (pause) **if**. Check work.
f. Repeat *a* through *e* for **it**.

TASK 3 Say the sounds, write sit, see, me, at, am

a. You're going to write the word (pause) **sit**. Say the sounds in **sit**. Get ready. Clap for each sound as the children say *sss* (pause) *iii* (pause) *t*. Repeat until firm.
b. Everybody, write the word (pause) **sit**. Check work.
c. Repeat *a* and *b* for **see, me, at,** and **am**.

> **Note:** Children who are placed at lesson 11 in the reading program begin at lesson 11 in the spelling program.

LESSON 11

SOUND WRITING

TASK 1 Write a, h, i, s, e

a. You're going to write some sounds.
b. Here's the first sound you're going to write. Listen. **aaa**. What sound? (Signal.) *aaa*.
c. Write **aaa**. Check work.
d. Next sound. Listen. **h**. What sound? (Signal.) *h*.
e. Write **h**. Check work.
f. Repeat *d* and *e* for **i, s,** and **e**.

TASK 2 Introduce sound combination th

a. Write on the board: **th**.
b. Point to **th**. Everybody, tell me the sound these letters make. Get ready. (Signal.) *th*. Yes, **th**.
c. Erase **th**. Everybody, write the letters that go together and make the sound **th**. Check work.

WORD WRITING

TASK 3 Read, say the sounds, write **sit**, **rat**

a. Write **sit** on the board.
b. Everybody, read this word the fast way. Get ready. (Signal.) *Sit*. What word? (Signal.) *Sit*. Yes, **sit**.
c. My turn to say the sounds in **sit** the hard way. Touch each sound. **Sss** (pause) **iii** (pause) **t**.
d. Your turn. Say the sounds in **sit** the hard way. Get ready. Touch each sound as children say *sss* (pause) *iii* (pause) *t*.
e. Erase **sit**. I'll clap for each sound. You say the sounds in **sit** the hard way. Get ready. Clap for each sound as children say *sss* (pause) *iii* (pause) *t*. Repeat until firm.
f. Everybody, write the word (pause) **sit**. Check work.
g. Repeat *a* through *f* for **rat**.

TASK 4 Read, say the sounds, write **man**, **fit**, **he**

a. Write **man** on the board.
b. Everybody, read this word the fast way. Get ready. (Signal.) *Man*. What word? (Signal.) *Man*. Yes, **man**.
c. Say the sounds in **man** the hard way. Touch each sound as the children say *mmm* (pause) *aaa* (pause) *nnn*.
d. Erase **man**. I'll clap for each sound. You say the sounds in **man** the hard way. Get ready. Clap for each sound as the children say *mmm* (pause) *aaa* (pause) *nnn*. Repeat until firm.
e. Everybody, write the word (pause) **man**. Check work.
f. Repeat *a* through *e* for **fit** and **he**.

LESSON 12

SOUND WRITING

TASK 1 Write **e, m, a, s, i**

a. You're going to write some sounds.
b. Here's the first sound you're going to write. Listen. **eee**. What sound? (Signal.) *eee*.
c. Write **eee**. Check work.
d. Next sound. Listen. **mmm**. What sound? (Signal.) *mmm*.
e. Write **mmm**. Check work.
f. Repeat *d* and *e* for **a, s,** and **i**.

WORD WRITING

TASK 2 Read, say the sounds, write **rat**

a. Write **rat** on the board.
b. Everybody, read this word the fast way. Get ready. (Signal.) *Rat*. What word? (Signal.) *Rat*. Yes, **rat**.
c. My turn to say the sounds in **rat** the hard way. Touch each sound. **Rrr** (pause) **aaa** (pause) **t**.
d. Your turn. Say the sounds in **rat** the hard way. Get ready. Touch each sound as children say *rrr* (pause) *aaa* (pause) *t*.
e. Erase **rat**. I'll clap for each sound. You say the sounds in **rat** the hard way. Get ready. Clap for each sound as children say *rrr* (pause) *aaa* (pause) *t*. Repeat until firm.
f. Everybody, write the word (pause) **rat**. Check work.

TASK 3 Read, say the sounds, write **sit**, **fit**

a. Write **sit** on the board.
b. Everybody, read this word the fast way. Get ready. (Signal.) *Sit*. What word? (Signal.) *Sit*. Yes, **sit**.
c. Say the sounds in **sit** the hard way. Touch each sound as the children say *sss* (pause) *iii* (pause) *t*.
d. Erase **sit**. I'll clap for each sound. You say the sounds in **sit** the hard way. Get ready. Clap for each sound as the children say *sss* (pause) *iii* (pause) *t*. Repeat until firm.
e. Everybody, write the word (pause) **sit**. Check work.
f. Repeat *a* through *e* for **fit**.

SOUND WRITING

TASK 4 Introduce sound combination **th**

a. Write on the board: **th**.
b. Point to **th**. Everybody, tell me the sound these letters make. Get ready. (Signal.) *th*. Yes, **th**.
c. Erase **th**. Everybody, write the letters that go together and make the sound **th**. Check work.

WORD WRITING

TASK 5 Write sound combination words **this**, **that**, **the**, **them**

a. Write on the board: **this, that, the, them.**
b. Point to **this. Everybody, read this word the fast way. Get ready.** (Signal.) *This.* **Yes, this.**
c. **Everybody, say the sounds you write for the word** (pause) **this. Get ready.** Touch **th, i, s** as the children say *th* (pause) *iii* (pause) *sss.* Repeat until firm.
d. Erase **this. Everybody, write the word** (pause) **this.** Check work.
e. Point to **that. Everybody, read this word the fast way. Get ready.** (Signal.) *That.* **Yes, that.**
f. **Everybody, say the sounds you write for the word** (pause) **that. Get ready.** Touch **th, a, t** as the children say *th* (pause) *aaa* (pause) *t.* Repeat until firm.
g. Erase **that. Everybody, write the word** (pause) **that.** Check work.
h. Point to **the. Everybody, read this word the fast way. Get ready.** (Signal.) *The.* **Yes, the.**
i. **Everybody, say the sounds you write for the word** (pause) **the. Get ready.** Touch **th, e** as the children say *th* (pause) $\bar{e}\bar{e}\bar{e}.$ Repeat until firm.
j. Erase **the. Everybody, write the word** (pause) **the.** Check work.
k. Point to **them. Everybody, read this word the fast way. Get ready.** (Signal.) *Them.* **Yes, them.**
l. **Everybody, say the sounds you write for the word** (pause) **them. Get ready.** Touch **th, e, m** as the children say *th* (pause) *eee* (pause) *mmm.*
m. Erase **them. Everybody, write the word** (pause) **them.** Check work.

LESSON 13

SOUND WRITING

TASK 1   Write **a, h, i, s, e**

a. **You're going to write some sounds.**
b. **Here's the first sound you're going to write. Listen. aaa. What sound?** (Signal.) *aaa.*
c. **Write aaa.** Check work.
d. **Next sound. Listen. h. What sound?** (Signal.) *h.*
e. **Write h.** Check work.
f. Repeat *d* and *e* for **i, s,** and **e.**

TASK 2   Introduce sound combination **th**

a. Write on the board: **th.**
b. Point to **th. Everybody, tell me the sound these letters make. Get ready.** (Signal.) *th.* **Yes, th.**
c. Erase **th. Everybody, write the letters that go together and make the sound th.** Check work.

WORD WRITING

TASK 3   Write sound combination words **that, the, this, them**

a. Write on the board: **that, the, this, them.**
b. Point to **that. Everybody, read this word the fast way. Get ready.** (Signal.) *That.* **Yes, that.**
c. **Everybody, say the sounds you write for the word** (pause) **that. Get ready.** Touch **th, a, t** as the children say *th* (pause) *aaa* (pause) *t.* Repeat until firm.
d. Erase **that. Everybody, write the word** (pause) **that.** Check work.

e. Point to **the. Everybody, read this word the fast way. Get ready.** (Signal.) *The.* **Yes, the.**
f. **Everybody, say the sounds you write for the word** (pause) **the. Get ready.** Touch **th, e** as the children say *th* (pause) $\bar{e}\bar{e}\bar{e}.$ Repeat until firm.
g. Erase **the. Everybody, write the word** (pause) **the.** Check work.
h. Point to **this. Everybody, read this word the fast way. Get ready.** (Signal.) *This.* **Yes, this.**
i. **Everybody, say the sounds you write for the word** (pause) **this. Get ready.** Touch **th, i, s** as the children say *th* (pause) *iii* (pause) *sss.* Repeat until firm.
j. Erase **this. Everybody, write the word** (pause) **this.** Check work.
k. Point to **them. Everybody, read this word the fast way. Get ready.** (Signal.) *Them.* **Yes, them.**
l. **Everybody, say the sounds you write for the word** (pause) **them. Get ready.** Touch **th, e, m** as the children say *th* (pause) *eee* (pause) *mmm.* Repeat until firm.
m. Erase **them. Everybody, write the word** (pause) **them.** Check work.

TASK 4   Say the sounds, write **he, me, hat, hit**

a. **You're going to write the word** (pause) **he. Say the sounds in he. Get ready.** Clap for each sound as the children say *h* (pause) $\bar{e}\bar{e}\bar{e}.$ Repeat until firm.
b. **Everybody, write the word** (pause) **he.** Check work.
c. Repeat *a* and *b* for **me, hat,** and **hit.**

LESSON 14

SOUND WRITING

TASK 1   Write r, t, f

a. You're going to write some sounds.
b. Here's the first sound you're going to write. Listen. **rrr**. What sound? (Signal.) *rrr*.
c. Write **rrr**. Check work.
d. Next sound. Listen. **t**. What sound? (Signal.) *t*.
e. Write **t**. Check work.
f. Repeat *d* and *e* for **f**.

TASK 2   Write th

a. Everybody, you're going to write the letters that go together and make the sound **th**. What sound? (Signal.) *th*.
b. Write **th**. Check work.

WORD WRITING

TASK 3   Write sound combination words the, them, that, this

a. Write on the board: **the, them, that, this**
b. Point to **the**. Everybody, read this word the fast way. Get ready. (Signal.) *The*. Yes, **the**.

c. Everybody, say the sounds you write for the word (pause) **the**. Get ready. Touch **th, e** as the children say *th* (pause) *ēēē*. Repeat until firm.
d. Erase **the**. Everybody, write the word (pause) **the**. Check work.
e. Repeat *b* through *d* for **them, that**, and **this**.

TASK 4   Say the sounds, write ran, him, he, we, fan

a. You're going to write the word (pause) **ran**. Say the sounds in **ran**. Get ready. Clap for each sound as the children say *rrr* (pause) *aaa* (pause) *nnn*. Repeat until firm.
b. Everybody, write the word (pause) **ran**. Check work.
c. Repeat *a* and *b* for **him, he, we**, and **fan**.

LESSON 15

SOUND WRITING

TASK 1   Write f, t, d

a. You're going to write some sounds.
b. Here's the first sound you're going to write. Listen. **fff**. What sound? (Signal.) *fff*.
c. Write **fff**. Check work.
d. Next sound. Listen. **t**. What sound? (Signal.) *t*.
e. Write **t**. Check work.
f. Repeat *d* and *e* for **d**.

TASK 2   Write th

a. Everybody, you're going to write the letters that go together and make the sound **th**. What sound? (Signal.) *th*.
b. Write **th**. Check work.

WORD WRITING

TASK 3   Write sound combination words them, this, that, the

a. Write on the board: **them, this, that, the**.
b. Point to **them**. Everybody, read this word the fast way. Get ready. (Signal.) *Them*. Yes, **them**.
c. Everybody, say the sounds you write for the word (pause) **them**. Get ready. Touch **th, e, m** as the children say *th* (pause) *eee* (pause) *mmm*. Repeat until firm.
d. Erase **them**. Everybody, write the word (pause) **them**. Check work.
e. Repeat *b* through *d* for **this, that**, and **the**.

TASK 4   Say the sounds, write fit, we

a. You're going to write the word (pause) **fit**. Say the sounds in **fit**. Get ready. Clap for each sound as the children say *fff* (pause) *iii* (pause) *t*. Repeat until firm.
b. Everybody, write the word (pause) **fit**. Check work.
c. Repeat *a* and *b* for **we**.

TASK 5   Write fat, him, ham

a. You're going to write the word (pause) **fat**. Think about the sounds in **fat** and write the word. Check work.
b. Repeat *a* for **him** and **ham**.

LESSON 16

SOUND WRITING

TASK 1   Write d, p, t, f

a. You're going to write some sounds.
b. Here's the first sound you're going to write. Listen. **d**. What sound? (Signal.) *d.*
c. Write **d**. Check work.
d. Next sound. Listen. **p**. What sound? (Signal.) *p.*
e. Write **p**. Check work.
f. Repeat *d* and *e* for **t** and **f**.

TASK 2   Write th

a. Everybody, you're going to write the letters that go together and make the sound **th**. What sound? (Signal.) *th.*
b. Write **th**. Check work.

WORD WRITING

TASK 3   Say the sounds, write he, that, fan, fin

a. You're going to write the word (pause) **he**. Say the sounds in **he**. Get ready. Clap for each sound as the children say *h* (pause) *ēēē*. Repeat until firm.
b. Everybody, write the word (pause) **he**. Check work.
c. Repeat *a* and *b* for **that, fan,** and **fin**.

TASK 4   Write me, this, him, ham, mat, sat, sit

a. You're going to write the word (pause) **me**. Think about the sounds in **me** and write the word. Check work.
b. Repeat *a* for **this, him, ham, mat, sat,** and **sit**.

LESSON 17

SOUND WRITING

TASK 1   Write r, d, p, g

a. You're going to write some sounds.
b. Here's the first sound you're going to write. Listen. **rrr**. What sound? (Signal.) *rrr.*
c. Write **rrr**. Check work.
d. Next sound. Listen. **d**. What sound? (Signal.) *d.*
e. Write **d**. Check work.
f. Repeat *d* and *e* for **p** and **g**.

TASK 2   Introduce sound combination ar

a. Write on the board: **ar**.
b. Point to **ar**. Everybody, tell me the sound these letters make. Get ready. (Signal.) *Are.* Yes, **are**.
c. Erase **ar**. Everybody, write the letters that go together and make the sound **are**. Check work.

WORD WRITING

TASK 3   Write sound combination words far, tar, car

a. Write on the board: **far, tar, car**.
b. Point to **far**. Everybody, read this word the fast way. Get ready. (Signal.) *Far.* Yes, **far**.
c. Everybody, say the sounds you write for the word (pause) **far**. Get ready. Touch **f, ar** as the children say *fff* (pause) *ar*. Repeat until firm.
d. Erase **far**. Everybody, write the word (pause) **far**. Check work.
e. Repeat *b* through *d* for **tar** and **car**.

TASK 4   Say the sounds, write that, this, the

a. You're going to write the word (pause) **that**. Say the sounds in **that**. Get ready. Clap for each sound as the children say *th* (pause) *aaa* (pause) *t*. Repeat until firm.
b. Everybody, write the word (pause) **that**. Check work.
c. Repeat *a* and *b* for **this** and **the**.

TASK 5   Write ham, him, me, sit, sat

a. You're going to write the word (pause) **ham**. Think about the sounds in **ham** and write the word. Check work.
b. Repeat *a* for **him, me, sit,** and **sat**.

LESSON 18

SOUND WRITING

TASK 1   Write m, n, b, g

a. You're going to write some sounds.
b. Here's the first sound you're going to write. Listen. **mmm**. What sound? (Signal.) *mmm.*
c. Write **mmm**. Check work.
d. Next sound. Listen. **nnn**. What sound? (Signal.) *nnn.*
e. Write **nnn**. Check work.
f. Repeat *d* and *e* for **b** and **g**.

TASK 2   Introduce sound combination ar

a. Write on the board: **ar**.
b. Point to **ar**. Everybody, tell me the sound these letters make. Get ready. (Signal.) *Are.* Yes, **are**.
c. Erase **ar**. Everybody, write the letters that go together and make the sound **are**. Check work.

WORD WRITING

TASK 3   Write sound combination words bar, barn, far, farm

a. Write on the board: **bar, barn, far, farm**.
b. Point to **bar**. Everybody, read this word the fast way. Get ready. (Signal.) *Bar.* Yes, **bar**.
c. Everybody, say the sounds you write for the word (pause) **bar**. Get ready. Touch **b, ar** as the children say *b* (pause) *ar.* Repeat until firm.

d. Erase **bar**. Everybody, write the word (pause) **bar**. Check work.
e. Repeat *b* through *d* for **barn, far,** and **farm**.

TASK 4   Say the sounds, write sat, hat, fin

a. You're going to write the word (pause) **sat**. Say the sounds in **sat**. Get ready. Clap for each sound as the children say *sss* (pause) *aaa* (pause) *t.* Repeat until firm.
b. Everybody, write the word (pause) **sat**. Check work.
c. Repeat *a* and *b* for **hat** and **fin**.

TASK 5   Write that, this, sit

a. You're going to write the word (pause) **that**. Think about the sounds in **that** and write the word. Check work.
b. Repeat *a* for **this** and **sit**.

LESSON 19

SOUND WRITING

TASK 1   Write e, a, m, b

a. You're going to write some sounds.
b. Here's the first sound you're going to write. Listen. **eee**. What sound? (Signal.) *eee.*
c. Write **eee**. Check work.
d. Next sound. Listen. **aaa**. What sound? (Signal.) *aaa.*
e. Write **aaa**. Check work.
f. Repeat *d* and *e* for **m** and **b**.

TASK 2   Write ar

a. Everybody, you're going to write the letters that go together and make the sound **are**. What sound? (Signal.) *Are.*
b. Write **are**. Check work.

WORD WRITING

TASK 3   Write sound combination words far, bar, farm, barn

a. Write on the board: **far, bar, farm, barn**.
b. Point to **far**. Everybody, read this word the fast way. Get ready. (Signal.) *Far.* Yes, **far**.
c. Everybody, say the sounds you write for the word (pause) **far**. Get ready. Touch **f, ar** as the children say *fff* (pause) *ar.* Repeat until firm.
d. Erase **far**. Everybody, write the word (pause) **far**. Check work.
e. Repeat *b* through *d* for **bar, farm,** and **barn**.

TASK 4   Say the sounds, write if, it, sit, that

a. You're going to write the word (pause) **if**. Say the sounds in **if**. Get ready. Clap for each sound as the children say *iii* (pause) *fff.* Repeat until firm.
b. Everybody, write the word (pause) **if**. Check work.
c. Repeat *a* and *b* for **it, sit,** and **that**.

TASK 5 Write **sat, hat, the**

a. You're going to write the word (pause)
   sat. Think about the sounds in **sat** and
   write the word.   Check work.
b. Repeat *a* for **hat** and **the**.

LESSON 20

SOUND WRITING

TASK 1 Write **e, n, i, d**

a. You're going to write some sounds.
b. Here's the first sound you're going to
   write. Listen. **eee**. What sound? (Signal.)
   eee.
c. Write **eee**. Check work.
d. Next sound. Listen. **nnn**. What sound?
   (Signal.) *nnn*.
e. Write **nnn**. Check work.
f. Repeat *d* and *e* for **i** and **d**.

TASK 2 Write **ar**

a. Everybody, you're going to write the
   letters that go together and make the
   sound **are**. What sound? (Signal.) *Are*.
b. Write **are**. Check work.

WORD WRITING

TASK 3 Write sound combination words **barn, car, arm, farm**

a. Write on the board: **barn, car, arm, farm**.
b. Point to **barn**. Everybody, read this word
   the fast way. Get ready. (Signal.) *Barn*.
   Yes, **barn**.
c. Everybody, say the sounds you write for
   the word (pause) **barn**. Get ready. Touch
   b, ar, n as the children say *b* (pause) *ar*
   (pause) *nnn*. Repeat until firm.
d. Erase **barn**. Everybody, write the word
   (pause) **barn**. Check work.
e. Repeat *b* through *d* for **car, arm,** and
   farm.

TASK 4 Say the sounds, write **cat, him, them**

a. You're going to write the word (pause)
   cat. Say the sounds in **cat**. Get ready.
   Clap for each sound as the children say *c*
   (pause) *aaa* (pause) *t*. Repeat until firm.
b. Everybody, write the word (pause) **cat**.
   Check work.
c. Repeat *a* and *b* for **him** and **them**.

TASK 5 Write **hat, ham, hit, sit, this**

a. You're going to write the word (pause)
   hat. Think about the sounds in **hat** and
   write the word. Check work.
b. Repeat *a* for **ham, hit, sit,** and **this**.

LESSON 21

SOUND WRITING

TASK 1 Write **e, i, r, a**

a. You're going to write some sounds.
b. Here's the first sound you're going to write.
   Listen. **eee**. What sound? (Signal.) *eee*.
c. Write **eee**. Check work.
d. Next sound. Listen. **iii**. What sound?
   (Signal.) *iii*.
e. Write **iii**. Check work.
f. Repeat *d* and *e* for **r** and **a**.

WORD WRITING

TASK 2 Listen, say the sounds, write **is, has**

a. You're going to write the word (pause) **is**.
   When you write the word **is**, you write
   these sounds: **iii** (pause) **sss**.
b. Say the sounds you write for (pause) **is**.
   Get ready. Clap for each sound as the
   children say *iii* (pause) *sss*. Repeat until firm.
c. Everybody, write the word (pause) **is**.
   Check work.
d. Repeat *a* through *c* for **has**.

TASK 3 Say the sounds, write **if, farm, tar, bat**

a. You're going to write the word (pause) **if**.
   Say the sounds in **if**. Get ready. Clap for
   each sound as the children say *iii* (pause) *fff*.
   Repeat until firm.
b. Everybody, write the word (pause) **if**.
   Check work.
c. Repeat *a* and *b* for **farm, tar,** and **bat**.

TASK 4 Write **arm, car, hat, me, we**

a. You're going to write the word (pause) **arm**. Think about the sounds in **arm** and write the word. Check work.
b. Repeat *a* for **car, hat, me,** and **we**.

SENTENCE WRITING

TASK 5 Write one sentence

Children are not responsible for capital letters.

a. Listen to this sentence. **He is fat.** Say that sentence. Get ready. (Signal.) *He is fat.*
b. Now you're going to say that sentence the slow way. Get ready. (Signal.) Signal for each word as the children say, *He* (pause) *is* (pause) *fat.*
c. Everybody, write the sentence. Spell each word the right way. Remember to put a period at the end of your sentence. Check work.

LESSON 22

SOUND WRITING

TASK 1 Write **o, e, c, p**

a. You're going to write some sounds.
b. Here's the first sound you're going to write. Listen. **ooo.** What sound? (Signal.) *ooo.*
c. Write **ooo.** Check work.
d. Next sound. Listen. **eee.** What sound? (Signal.) *eee.*
e. Write **eee.** Check work.
f. Repeat *d* and *e* for **c** and **p**.

WORD WRITING

TASK 2 Say the sounds, write **this, far, we, barn, is, has**

a. You're going to write the word (pause) **this.** Say the sounds in **this.** Get ready. Clap for each sound as the children say *th* (pause) *iii* (pause) *sss.* Repeat until firm.
b. Everybody, write the word (pause) **this.** Check work.
c. Repeat *a* and *b* for **far, we, barn, is,** and **has.**

TASK 3 Write **hat, sit, tar, it, that, me, if**

a. You're going to write the word (pause) **hat.** Think about the sounds in **hat** and write the word. Check work.
b. Repeat *a* for **sit, tar, it, that, me,** and **if.**

SENTENCE WRITING

TASK 4 Write one sentence

a. Listen to this sentence. **He is a man.** Say that sentence. Get ready. (Signal.) *He is a man.*
b. Now you're going to say that sentence the slow way. Get ready. (Signal.) Signal for each word as the children say, *He* (pause) *is* (pause) *a* (pause) *man.*
c. Everybody, write the sentence. Spell each word the right way. Remember to put a period at the end of your sentence. Check work.

LESSON 23

SOUND WRITING

TASK 1 Write **o, b, m, n**

a. You're going to write some sounds.
b. Here's the first sound you're going to write. Listen. **ooo.** What sound? (Signal.) *ooo.*
c. Write **ooo.** Check work.
d. Next sound. Listen. **b.** What sound? (Signal.) *b.*
e. Write **b.** Check work.
f. Repeat *d* and *e* for **m** and **n.**

TASK 2 Introduce sound combination **sh**

a. Write on the board: **sh.**
b. Point to **sh.** Everybody, tell me the sound these letters make. Get ready. (Signal.) *sh.* Yes, **sh.**
c. Erase **sh.** Everybody, write the letters that go together and make the sound **sh.** Check work.

WORD WRITING

TASK 3 Say the sounds, write **bad, him, arm, men, ten, set**

a. You're going to write the word (pause) **bad.** Say the sounds in **bad.** Get ready. Clap for each sound as the children say *b* (pause) *aaa* (pause) *d.* Repeat until firm.
b. Everybody, write the word (pause) **bad.** Check work.
c. Repeat *a* and *b* for **him, arm, men, ten,** and **set.**

TASK 4 Write **met, bar, farm, sad, has**

a. You're going to write the word (pause) **met**. Think about the sounds in **met** and write the word. Check work.
b. Repeat *a* for **bar, farm, sad,** and **has**.

SENTENCE WRITING

TASK 5 Write one sentence

a. Listen to this sentence.
   He is a fat man.
   Say that sentence. Get ready. (Signal.)
   He is a fat man.
b. Now you're going to say that sentence the slow way. Get ready. (Signal.) Signal for each word as the children say, *He* (pause) *is* (pause) *a* (pause) *fat* (pause) *man.*
c. Everybody, write the sentence. Spell each word the right way. Remember to put a period at the end of your sentence. Check work.

LESSON 24

SOUND WRITING

TASK 1 Write **o, e, g, f**

a. You're going to write some sounds.
b. Here's the first sound you're going to write. Listen. **ooo**. What sound? (Signal.) *ooo.*
c. Write **ooo**. Check work.
d. Next sound. Listen. **eee**. What sound? (Signal.) *eee.*
e. Write **eee**. Check work.
f. Repeat *d* and *e* for **g** and **f**.

TASK 2 Introduce sound combination **sh**

a. Write on the board: **sh**.
b. Point to **sh**. Everybody, tell me the sound these letters make. Get ready. (Signal.) *sh.* Yes, **sh**.
c. Erase **sh**. Everybody, write the letters that go together and make the sound **sh**. Check work.

WORD WRITING

TASK 3 Write sound combination words **she, wish, ship**

a. Write on the board: **she, wish, ship**.
b. Point to **she**. Everybody, read this word the fast way. Get ready. (Signal.) *She.* Yes, **she**.
c. Everybody, say the sounds you write for the word (pause) **she**. Get ready. Touch **sh, e** as the children say *sh* (pause) *ēēē.* Repeat until firm.
d. Erase **she**. Everybody, write the word (pause) **she**. Check work.
e. Repeat *b* through *d* for **wish** and **ship**.

TASK 4 Listen, say the sounds, write **will**

a. You're going to write the word (pause) **will**. When you write the word **will**, you write these sounds: **www** (pause) **iii** (pause) **lll** (pause) **lll**.
b. Say the sounds you write for (pause) **will**. Get ready. Clap for each sound as the children say *www* (pause) *iii* (pause) *lll* (pause) *lll*. Repeat until firm.
c. Everybody, write the word (pause) **will**. Check work.

TASK 5 Say the sounds, write **did, met, bet**

a. You're going to write the word (pause) **did**. Say the sounds in **did**. Get ready. Clap for each sound as the children say *d* (pause) *iii* (pause) *d*. Repeat until firm.
b. Everybody, write the word (pause) **did**. Check work.
c. Repeat *a* and *b* for **met** and **bet**.

TASK 6 Write **is, has, that, ran, bad, me**

a. You're going to write the word (pause) **is**. Think about the sounds in **is** and write the word. Check work.
b. Repeat *a* for **has, that, ran, bad,** and **me**.

SENTENCE WRITING

TASK 7 Write one sentence

a. Listen to this sentence.
   He has a cat.
   Say that sentence. Get ready. (Signal.)
   He has a cat.
b. Now you're going to say that sentence the slow way. Get ready. (Signal.) Signal for each word as the children say, *He* (pause) *has* (pause) *a* (pause) *cat.*
c. Everybody, write the sentence. Spell each word the right way. Check work.

LESSON 25

SOUND WRITING

TASK 1 Write e, r, o, c, d, t

a. You're going to write some sounds.
b. Here's the first sound you're going to write. Listen. **eee**. What sound? (Signal.) *eee*.
c. Write **eee**. Check work.
d. Next sound. Listen. **rrr**. What sound? (Signal.) *rrr*.
e. Write **rrr**. Check work.
f. Repead *d* and *e* for **o, c, d,** and **t**.

TASK 2 Introduce sound combination sh

a. Write on the board: **sh**.
b. Point to **sh**. Everybody, tell me the sound these letters make. Get ready. (Signal.) *sh*. Yes, **sh**.
c. Erase **sh**. Everybody, write the letters that go together and make the sound **sh**. Check work.

WORD WRITING

TASK 3 Write sound combination words ship, she, wish, fish

a. Write on the board: **ship, she, wish, fish.**
b. Point to **ship.** Everybody, read this word the fast way. Get ready. (Signal.) *Ship.* Yes, **ship.**
c. Everybody, say the sounds you write for the word (pause) **ship**. Get ready. Touch **sh, i, p** as the children say *sh* (pause) *iii* (pause) *p*. Repeat until firm.
d. Erase **ship.** Everybody, write the word (pause) **ship**. Check work.
e. Repeat *b* through *d* for **she, wish,** and **fish.**

TASK 4 Listen, say the sounds, write was, will

a. You're going to write the word (pause) **was**. When you write the word **was**, you write these sounds: **www** (pause) **aaa** (pause) **sss**.
b. Say the sounds you write for (pause) **was**. Get ready. Clap for each sound as the children say *www* (pause) *aaa* (pause) *sss*. Repeat until firm.
c. Everybody, write the word (pause) **was**. Check work.
d. Repeat *a* through *c* for **will.**

TASK 5 Say the sounds, write this, him, far

a. You're going to write the word (pause) **this**. Say the sounds in **this**. Get ready. Clap for each sound as the children say *th* (pause) *iii* (pause) *sss*. Repeat until firm.
b. Everybody, write the word (pause) **this**. Check work.
c. Repeat *a* and *b* for **him** and **far.**

TASK 6 Write did, hat, men

a. You're going to write the word (pause) **did**. Think about the sounds in **did** and write the word. Check work.
b. Repeat *a* for **hat** and **men.**

SENTENCE WRITING

TASK 7 Write one sentence

a. Listen to this sentence.
   He has a sad rat.
   Say that sentence. Get ready. (Signal.)
   He has a sad rat.
b. Now you're going to say that sentence the slow way. Get ready. (Signal.) Signal for each word as the children say, *He* (pause) *has* (pause) *a* (pause) *sad* (pause) *rat*.
c. Everybody, write the sentence. Spell each word the right way. Check work.

LESSON 26

SOUND WRITING

TASK 1 Write e, p, o, g, b, n

a. You're going to write some sounds.
b. Here's the first sound you're going to write. Listen. **eee**. What sound? (Signal.) *eee*.
c. Write **eee**. Check work.
d. Next sound. Listen. **p**. What sound? (Signal.) *p*.
e. Write **p**. Check work.
f. Repeat *d* and *e* for **o, g, b,** and **n**.

TASK 2 Write sh

a. Everybody, you're going to write the letters that go together and make the sound **sh**. What sound? (Signal.) *sh*.
b. Write **sh**. Check work.

WORD WRITING

TASK 3 Write sound combination words **she, fish, ship, dish**

a. Write on the board: **she, fish, ship, dish.**
b. Point to **she**. Everybody, read this word the fast way. Get ready. (Signal.) *She*. Yes, **she.**
c. Everybody, say the sounds you write for the word (pause) **she**. Get ready. Touch **sh, e** as the children say *sh* (pause) *ēēē*. Repeat until firm.
d. Erase **she**. Everybody, write the word (pause) **she**. Check work.
e. Repeat *b* through *d* for **fish, ship,** and **dish.**

TASK 4 Say the sounds, write **was, cop, top**

a. You're going to write the word (pause) **was**. Say the sounds in **was**. Get ready. Clap for each sound as the children say *www* (pause) *aaa* (pause) *sss*. Repeat until firm.
b. Everybody, write the word (pause) **was**. Check work.
c. Repeat *a* and *b* for **cop** and **top.**

TASK 5 Write **not, hot, barn, arm, then**

a. You're going to write the word (pause) **not**. Think about the sounds in **not** and write the word. Check work.
b. Repeat *a* for **hot, barn, arm,** and **then.**

SENTENCE WRITING

TASK 6 Write one sentence

a. Listen to this sentence.
   She has a ram.
   Say that sentence. Get ready. (Signal.) *She has a ram.*
b. Now you're going to say that sentence the slow way. Get ready. (Signal.) Signal for each word as the children say, *She* (pause) *has* (pause) *a* (pause) *ram.*
c. Everybody, write the sentence. Spell each word the right way. Check work.

LESSON 27

SOUND WRITING

TASK 1 Write **i, r, o, c, g, w**

a. You're going to write some sounds.
b. Here's the first sound you're going to write. Listen. **iii**. What sound? (Signal.) *iii.*
c. Write **iii**. Check work.
d. Next sound. Listen. **rrr**. What sound? (Signal.) *rrr.*
e. Write **rrr**. Check work.
f. Repeat *d* and *e* for **o, c, g,** and **w.**

TASK 2 Write **sh**

a. Everybody, you're going to write the letters that go together and make the sound **sh**. What sound? (Signal.) *sh.*
b. Write **sh**. Check work.

WORD WRITING

TASK 3 Write sound combination words **dish, ship, shop**

a. Write on the board: **dish, ship, shop.**
b. Point to **dish**. Everybody, read this word the fast way. Get ready. (Signal.) *Dish*. Yes, **dish.**
c. Everybody, say the sounds you write for the word (pause) **dish**. Get ready. Touch **d, i, sh** as the children say *d* (pause) *iii* (pause) *sh*. Repeat until firm.
d. Erase **dish**. Everybody, write the word (pause) **dish**. Check work.
e. Repeat *b* through *d* for **ship** and **shop.**

TASK 4 Say the sounds, write **car, was, has, is**

a. You're going to write the word (pause) **car**. Say the sounds in **car**. Get ready. Clap for each sound as the children say *c* (pause) *ar*. Repeat until firm.
b. Everybody, write the word (pause) **car**. Check work.
c. Repeat *a* and *b* for **was, has,** and **is.**

TASK 5 Write **we, he, not, hop, far, did, this**

a. You're going to write the word (pause) **we**. Think about the sounds in **we** and write the word. Check work.
b. Repeat *a* for **he, not, hop, far, did,** and **this.**

SENTENCE WRITING

TASK 6 Write one sentence

a. Listen to this sentence.
That cop has fish.
Say that sentence. Get ready. (Signal.)
That cop has fish.

b. Now you're going to say that sentence the slow way. Get ready. (Signal.) Signal for each word as the children say, *That* (pause) *cop* (pause) *has* (pause) *fish.*

c. Everybody, write the sentence. Spell each word the right way. Check work.

LESSON 28

SOUND WRITING

TASK 1 Write **e, n, m, c, p, l**

a. You're going to write some sounds.

b. Here's the first sound you're going to write. Listen. **eee**. What sound? (Signal.) *eee.*

c. Write **eee**. Check work.

d. Next sound. Listen. **nnn**. What sound? (Signal.) *nnn.*

e. Write **nnn**. Check work.

f. Repeat *d* and *e* for **m, c, p,** and **l**.

TASK 2 Write **ar, th, sh**

a. Everybody, you're going to write the letters that go together and make the sound **are**. What sound? (Signal.) *Are.*

b. Write **are**. Check work.

c. Repeat *a* and *b* for **th** and **sh**.

WORD WRITING

TASK 3 Say the sounds, write **shop, barn, wet, dish, will**

a. You're going to write the word (pause) **shop**. Say the sounds in **shop**. Get ready. Clap for each sound as the children say *sh* (pause) *ooo* (pause) *p*. Repeat until firm.

b. Everybody, write the word (pause) **shop**. Check work.

c. Repeat *a* and *b* for **barn, wet, dish,** and **will**.

TASK 4 Write **ten, met, fat, was, is, that, hat, hop, cop**

a. You're going to write the word (pause) **ten**. Think about the sounds in **ten** and write the word. Check work.

b. Repeat *a* for **met, fat, was, is, that, hat, hop,** and **cop**.

SENTENCE WRITING

TASK 5 Write one sentence

a. Listen to this sentence.
She is not sad.
Say that sentence. Get ready. (Signal.)
She is not sad.

b. Now you're going to say that sentence the slow way. Get ready. (Signal.) Signal for each word as the children say, *She* (pause) *is* (pause) *not* (pause) *sad.*

c. Everybody, write the sentence. Spell each word the right way. Check work.

LESSON 29

SOUND WRITING

TASK 1 Write **o, r, f, g**

a. You're going to write some sounds.

b. Here's the first sound you're going to write. Listen. **ooo**. What sound? (Signal.) *ooo.*

c. Write **ooo**. Check work.

d. Next sound. Listen. **rrr**. What sound? (Signal.) *rrr.*

e. Write **rrr**. Check work.

f. Repeat *d* and *e* for **f** and **g**.

TASK 2 Write **th, ar, sh**

a. Everybody, you're going to write the letters that go together and make the sound **th**. What sound? (Signal.) *th.*

b. Write **th**. Check work.

c. Repeat *a* and *b* for **ar** and **sh**.

WORD WRITING

TASK 3 Listen, say the sounds, write **his**

a. You're going to write the word (pause) **his**. When you write the word **his**, you write these sounds: **h** (pause) **iii** (pause) **sss**.

b. Say the sounds you write for (pause) **his**. Get ready. Clap for each sound as the children say *h* (pause) *iii* (pause) *sss*. Repeat until firm.

c. Everybody, write the word (pause) **his**. Check work.

TASK 4 Say the sounds, write **ship**, **wish**, **farm**, **him**, **then**

a. You're going to write the word (pause) **ship**. Say the sounds in **ship**. Get ready. Clap for each sound as the children say *sh* (pause) *iii* (pause) *p*. Repeat until firm.

b. Everybody, write the word (pause) **ship**. Check work.

c. Repeat *a* and *b* for **wish**, **farm**, **him**, and **then**.

TASK 5 Write **bet**, **wet**, **that**, **arm**, **cop**, **hop**, **shop**

a. You're going to write the word (pause) **bet**. Think about the sounds in **bet** and write the word. Check work.

b. Repeat *a* for **wet**, **that**, **arm**, **cop**, **hop**, and **shop**.

SENTENCE WRITING

TASK 6 Write one sentence

a. Listen to this sentence. **She did not shop**. Say that sentence. Get ready. (Signal.) *She did not shop*.

b. Now you're going to say that sentence the slow way. Get ready. (Signal.) Signal for each word as the children say, *She* (pause) *did* (pause) *not* (pause) *shop*.

c. Everybody, write the sentence. Spell each word the right way. Check work.

LESSON 30

SOUND WRITING

TASK 1 Write **e**, **u**, **d**, **t**

a. You're going to write some sounds.

b. Here's the first sound you're going to write. Listen. **eee**. What sound? (Signal.) *eee*.

c. Write **eee**. Check work.

d. Next sound. Listen. **uuu**. What sound? (Signal.) *uuu*.

e. Write **uuu**. Check work.

f. Repeat *d* and *e* for **d** and **t**.

TASK 2 Write **sh**, **ar**, **th**

a. Everybody, you're going to write the letters that go together and make the sound **sh**. What sound? (Signal.) *sh*.

b. Write **sh**. Check work.

c. Repeat *a* and *b* for **ar** and **th**.

WORD WRITING

TASK 3 Say the sounds, write **is**, **his**, **if**, **tar**, **them**, **set**

a. You're going to write the word (pause) **is**. Say the sounds in **is**. Get ready. Clap for each sound as the children say *iii* (pause) *sss*. Repeat until firm.

b. Everybody, write the word (pause) **is**. Check work.

c. Repeat *a* and *b* for **his**, **if**, **tar**, **them**, and **set**.

TASK 4 Write **bar**, **was**, **hot**, **met**, **this**

a. You're going to write the word (pause) **bar**. Think about the sounds in **bar** and write the word. Check work.

b. Repeat *a* for **was**, **hot**, **met**, and **this**.

SENTENCE WRITING

TASK 5 Write one sentence

a. Listen to this sentence. **We did not shop**. Say that sentence. Get ready. (Signal.) *We did not shop*.

b. Now you're going to say that sentence the slow way. Get ready. (Signal.) Signal for each word as the children say, *We* (pause) *did* (pause) *not* (pause) *shop*.

c. Everybody, write the sentence. Spell each word the right way. Check work.

LESSON 31

SOUND WRITING

TASK 1 Write **u**, **o**, **b**, **m**

a. You're going to write some sounds.

b. Here's the first sound you're going to write. Listen. **uuu**. What sound? (Signal.) *uuu*.

c. Write **uuu**. Check work.

d. Next sound. Listen. **ooo**. What sound? (Signal.) *ooo*.

e. Write **ooo**. Check work.

f. Repeat *d* and *e* for **b** and **m**.

TASK 2   Introduce sound combination **ing**

a. Write on the board: **ing.**
b. Point to **ing.**   Everybody, tell me the sound these letters make. Get ready. (Signal.) *ing.*   Yes, **ing.**
c. Erase **ing.**   Everybody, write the letters that go together and make the sound **ing.** Check work.

WORD WRITING

TASK 3   Say the sounds, write **has, his, mop, mat, went, wish**

a. You're going to write the word (pause) **has.** Say the sounds in **has.** Get ready. Clap for each sound as the children say *h* (pause) *aaa* (pause) *sss.* Repeat until firm.
b. Everybody, write the word (pause) **has.** Check work.
c. Repeat *a* and *b* for **his, mop, mat, went,** and **wish.**

TASK 4   Write **far, barn, we, it, then, bad**

a. You're going to write the word (pause) **far.** Think about the sounds in **far** and write the word. Check work.
b. Repeat *a* for **barn, we, it, then,** and **bad.**

SENTENCE WRITING

TASK 5   Write one sentence

a. Listen to this sentence. **That dish was hot.** Say that sentence. Get ready. (Signal.) *That dish was hot.*
b. Now you're going to say that sentence the slow way. Get ready. (Signal.) Signal for each word as the children say, *That* (pause) *dish* (pause) *was* (pause) *hot.*
c. Everybody, write the sentence. Spell each word the right way. Check work.

LESSON 32

SOUND WRITING

TASK 1   Write **u, n, e, c**

a. You're going to write some sounds.
b. Here's the first sound you're going to write. Listen. **uuu.** What sound? (Signal.) *uuu.*
c. Write **uuu.** Check work.
d. Next sound. Listen. **nnn.** What sound? (Signal.) *nnn.*
e. Write **nnn.** Check work.
f. Repeat *d* and *e* for **e** and **c.**

TASK 2   Introduce sound combination **ing**

a. Write on the board: **ing.**
b. Point to **ing.**   Everybody, tell me the sound these letters make. Get ready. (Signal.) *ing.*   Yes, **ing.**
c. Erase **ing.**   Everybody, write the letters that go together and make the sound **ing.** Check work.

WORD WRITING

TASK 3   Write sound combination words **ring, sing, thing**

a. Write on the board: **ring, sing, thing.**
b. Point to **ring.**   Everybody, read this word the fast way. Get ready. (Signal.) *Ring.* Yes, **ring.**
c. Everybody, say the sounds you write for the word (pause) **ring.** Get ready. Touch **r, ing** as the children say *rrr* (pause) *ing.* Repeat until firm.
d. Erase **ring.**   Everybody, write the word (pause) **ring.** Check work.
e. Repeat *b* through *d* for **sing** and **thing.**

TASK 4   Say the sounds, write **cow, how, now, went**

a. You're going to write the word (pause) **cow.** Say the sounds in **cow.** Get ready. Clap for each sound as the children say *c* (pause) *ooo* (pause) *www.* Repeat until firm.
b. Everybody, write the word (pause) **cow.** Check work.
c. Repeat *a* and *b* for **how, now,** and **went.**

TASK 5   Write **car, farm, if, him, ship**

a. You're going to write the word (pause) **car.** Think about the sounds in **car** and write the word. Check work.
b. Repeat *a* for **farm, if, him,** and **ship.**

SENTENCE WRITING

TASK 6   Write one sentence

a. Listen to this sentence.
A fish was in a dish.
Say that sentence. Get ready. (Signal.)
A fish was in a dish.
b. Now you're going to say that sentence the slow way. Get ready. (Signal.) Signal for each word as the children say, *A* (pause) *fish* (pause) *was* (pause) *in* (pause) *a* (pause) *dish.*
c. Everybody, write the sentence. Spell each word the right way. Check work.

LESSON 33

SOUND WRITING

TASK 1   Write e, d, o, t

a. You're going to write some sounds.
b. Here's the first sound you're going to write. Listen. **eee.** What sound? (Signal.) *eee.*
c. Write **eee.** Check work.
d. Next sound. Listen. **d.** What sound? (Signal.) *d.*
e. Write **d.** Check work.
f. Repeat *d* and *e* for **o** and **t.**

TASK 2   Write ing

a. Everybody, you're going to write the letters that go together and make the sound **ing.** What sound? (Signal.) *ing.*
b. Write **ing.** Check work.

WORD WRITING

TASK 3   Write sound combination words sing, thing, ring

a. Write on the board: **sing, thing, ring.**
b. Point to **sing.** Everybody, read this word the fast way. Get ready. (Signal.) *Sing.* Yes, **sing.**
c. Everybody, say the sounds you write for the word (pause) **sing.** Get ready. Touch **s, ing** as the children say *sss* (pause) *ing.* Repeat until firm.
d. Erase **sing.** Everybody, write the word (pause) **sing.** Check work.
e. Repeat *b* through *d* for **thing** and **ring.**

TASK 4   Listen, say the sounds, write on

a. You're going to write the word (pause) **on.** When you write the word **on**, you write these sounds: **ooo** (pause) **nnn.**
b. Say the sounds you write for (pause) **on.** Get ready. Clap for each sound as the children say *ooo* (pause) *nnn.* Repeat until firm.
c. Everybody, write the word (pause) **on.** Check work.

TASK 5   Say the sounds, write hen, went, dug, bug, run, sun

a. You're going to write the word (pause) **hen.** Say the sounds in **hen.** Get ready. Clap for each sound as the children say *h* (pause) *eee* (pause) *nnn.* Repeat until firm.
b. Everybody, write the word (pause) **hen.** Check work.
c. Repeat *a* and *b* for **went, dug, bug, run, and sun.**

TASK 6   Write how, will, has

a. You're going to write the word (pause) **how.** Think about the sounds in **how** and write the word. Check work.
b. Repeat *a* for **will** and **has.**

SENTENCE WRITING

TASK 7   Write one sentence

a. Listen to this sentence. **The cow was in the barn.** Say that sentence. Get ready. (Signal.) *The cow was in the barn.*
b. Now you're going to say that sentence the slow way. Get ready. (Signal.) Signal for each word as the children say, *The* (pause) *cow* (pause) *was* (pause) *in* (pause) *the* (pause) *barn.*
c. Everybody, write the sentence. Spell each word the right way. Check work.

LESSON 34

SOUND WRITING

TASK 1   Write u, o, g, b

a. You're going to write some sounds.
b. Here's the first sound you're going to write. Listen. **uuu.** What sound? (Signal.) *uuu.*
c. Write **uuu.** Check work.
d. Next sound. Listen. **ooo.** What sound? (Signal.) *ooo.*
e. Write **ooo.** Check work.
f. Repeat *d* and *e* for **g** and **b.**

WORD WRITING

TASK 2 Say the sounds, write **thing**, **shop**, **park**

a. You're going to write the word (pause) **thing**. Say the sounds in **thing**. Get ready. Clap for each sound as the children say *th* (pause) *ing*. Repeat until firm.

b. Everybody, write the word (pause) **thing**. Check work.

c. Repeat *a* and *b* for **shop** and **park**.

TASK 3 Write **cop**, **wish**, **far**, **ring**, **rug**, **fun**, **bug**, **now**, **how**

a. You're going to write the word (pause) **cop**. Think about the sounds in **cop** and write the word. Check work.

b. Repeat *a* for **wish**, **far**, **ring**, **rug**, **fun**, **bug**, **now**, and **how**.

SENTENCE WRITING

TASK 4 Write one sentence

a. Listen to this sentence. **A hen was on a farm**. Say that sentence. Get ready. (Signal.) *A hen was on a farm.*

b. Now you're going to say that sentence the slow way. Get ready. (Signal.) Signal for each word as the children say, *A* (pause) *hen* (pause) *was* (pause) *on* (pause) *a* (pause) *farm.*

c. Everybody, write the sentence. Spell each word the right way. Check work.

LESSON 35

SOUND WRITING

TASK 1 Write **u**, **o**, **p**, **f**

a. You're going to write some sounds.

b. Here's the first sound you're going to write. Listen. **uuu**. What sound? (Signal.) *uuu.*

c. Write **uuu**. Check work.

d. Next sound. Listen. **ooo**. What sound? (Signal.) *ooo.*

e. Write **ooo**. Check work.

f. Repeat *d* and *e* for **p** and **f**.

WORD WRITING

TASK 2 Listen, say the sounds, write **to**, **do**

a. You're going to write the word (pause) **to**. When you write the word **to**, you write these sounds: **t** (pause) **ooo**.

b. Say the sounds you write for (pause) **to**. Get ready. Clap for each sound as the children say *t* (pause) *ooo*. Repeat until firm.

c. Everybody, write the word (pause) **to**. Check work.

d. Repeat *a* through *c* for **do**.

TASK 3 Say the sounds, write **if**, **cow**, **dark**, **sing**

a. You're going to write the word (pause) **if**. Say the sounds in **if**. Get ready. Clap for each sound as the children say *iii* (pause) *fff*. Repeat until firm.

b. Everybody, write the word (pause) **if**. Check work.

c. Repeat *a* and *b* for **cow**, **dark**, and **sing**.

TASK 4 Write **on**, **hen**, **then**, **now**, **dug**, **run**, **sun**

a. You're going to write the word (pause) **on**. Think about the sounds in **on** and write the word. Check work.

b. Repeat *a* for **hen**, **then**, **now**, **dug**, **run**, and **sun**.

SENTENCE WRITING

TASK 5 Write one sentence

a. Listen to this sentence. **She was in the park**. Say that sentence. Get ready. (Signal.) *She was in the park.*

b. Now you're going to say that sentence the slow way. Get ready. (Signal.) Signal for each word as the children say, *She* (pause) *was* (pause) *in* (pause) *the* (pause) *park.*

c. Everybody, write the sentence. Spell each word the right way. Check work.

LESSON 36

WORD WRITING

TASK 1 Say the sounds, write **to**, **do**, **bag**, **and**, **dig**, **ship**, **shop**

a. You're going to write the word (pause) **to**. Say the sounds in **to**. Get ready. Clap for each sound as the children say *t* (pause) *ooo*. Repeat until firm.

b. Everybody, write the word (pause) **to**. Check work.

c. Repeat *a* and *b* for **do**, **bag**, **and**, **dig**, **ship**, and **shop**.

TASK 2 Write **far, thing, has, how**

a. You're going to write the word (pause) **far**. Think about the sounds in **far** and write the word. Check work.

b. Repeat a for **thing, has,** and **how**.

SENTENCE WRITING

TASK 3 Write two sentences

a. Listen to this sentence.
The park was not dark.
Say that sentence. Get ready. (Signal.)
The park was not dark.

b. Now you're going to say that sentence the slow way. Get ready. (Signal.) Signal for each word as the children say, *The* (pause) *park* (pause) *was* (pause) *not* (pause) *dark.*

c. Everybody, write the sentence. Spell each word the right way. Check work.

d. Repeat a through c for **He has a cat.**

LESSON 37

WORD WRITING

TASK 1 Say the sounds, write **ring, dog, met, him**

a. You're going to write the word (pause) **ring**. Say the sounds in **ring**. Get ready. Clap for each sound as the children say *rrr* (pause) *ing*. Repeat until firm.

b. Everybody, write the word (pause) **ring**. Check work.

c. Repeat a and b for **dog, met,** and **him**.

TASK 2 Write **went, that, bark, bug, cop, has, big, how**

a. You're going to write the word (pause) **went**. Think about the sounds in **went** and write the word. Check work.

b. Repeat a for **that, bark, bug, cop, has, big,** and **how**.

SENTENCE WRITING

TASK 3 Write two sentences

a. Listen to this sentence.
His fish was not fat.
Say that sentence. Get ready. (Signal.)
His fish was not fat.

b. Now you're going to say that sentence the slow way. Get ready. (Signal.) Signal for each word as the children say, *His* (pause) *fish* (pause) *was* (pause) *not* (pause) *fat.*

c. Everybody, write the sentence. Spell each word the right way. Check work.

d. Repeat a through c for **She is fat and sad.**

LESSON 38

WORD WRITING

TASK 1 Say the sounds, write **can, if, do, us, get, set**

a. You're going to write the word (pause) **can**. Say the sounds in **can**. Get ready. Clap for each sound as the children say *c* (pause) *aaa* (pause) *nnn*. Repeat until firm.

b. Everybody, write the word (pause) **can**. Check work.

c. Repeat a and b for **if, do, us, get,** and **set**.

TASK 2 Write **to, has, sing, far, rug, ship, shop**

a. You're going to write the word (pause) **to**. Think about the sounds in **to** and write the word. Check work.

b. Repeat a for **has, sing, far, rug, ship,** and **shop**.

SENTENCE WRITING

TASK 3 Write two sentences

a. Listen to this sentence.
His hat is not wet.
Say that sentence. Get ready. (Signal.)
His hat is not wet.

b. Now you're going to say that sentence the slow way. Get ready. (Signal.) Signal for each word as the children say, *His* (pause) *hat* (pause) *is* (pause) *not* (pause) *wet.*

c. Everybody, write the sentence. Spell each word the right way. Check work.

d. Repeat a through c for **We will run and hop.**

LESSON 39

WORD WRITING

TASK 1 Listen, say the sounds, write **come**

a. You're going to write the word (pause) **come**. When you write the word **come**, you write these sounds: **c** (pause) **ooo** (pause) **mmm** (pause) **ēēē**.

b. Say the sounds you write for (pause) **come**. Get ready. Clap for each sound as the children say *c* (pause) *ooo* (pause) *mmm* (pause) *ēēē*. Repeat until firm.

c. Everybody, write the word (pause) **come**. Check work.

TASK 2 Say the sounds, write **bag, bug, thing, with**

a. You're going to write the word (pause) **bag.** Say the sounds in **bag.** Get ready. Clap for each sound as the children say *b* (pause) *aaa* (pause) *g.* Repeat until firm.
b. Everybody, write the word (pause) **bag.** Check work.
c. Repeat *a* and *b* for **bug, thing,** and **with.**

TASK 3 Write **sing, do, us, car, get, in**

a. You're going to write the word (pause) **sing.** Think about the sounds in **sing** and write the word. Check work.
b. Repeat *a* for **do, us, car, get,** and **in.**

SENTENCE WRITING

TASK 4 Write two sentences

a. Listen to this sentence.
   He has a cat and a rat.
   Say that sentence. Get ready. (Signal.)
   He has a cat and a rat.
b. Now you're going to say that sentence the slow way. Get ready. (Signal.) Signal for each word as the children say, *He* (pause) *has* (pause) *a* (pause) *cat* (pause) *and* (pause) *a* (pause) *rat.*
c. Everybody, write the sentence. Spell each word the right way. Check work.
d. Repeat *a* through *c* for **The cop was in the park.**

LESSON 40

WORD WRITING

TASK 1 Listen, say the sounds, write **come**

a. You're going to write the word (pause) **come.** When you write the word **come,** you write these sounds: **c** (pause) **ooo** (pause) **mmm** (pause) **ēēē.**
b. Say the sounds you write for (pause) **come.** Get ready. Clap for each sound as the children say *c* (pause) *ooo* (pause) *mmm* (pause) *ēēē.* Repeat until firm.
c. Everybody, write the word (pause) **come.** Check work.

TASK 2 Say the sounds, write **how, cow, with**

a. You're going to write the word (pause) **how.** Say the sounds in **how.** Get ready. Clap for each sound as the children say *h* (pause) *ooo* (pause) *www.* Repeat until firm.
b. Everybody, write the word (pause) **how.** Check work.
c. Repeat *a* and *b* for **cow** and **with.**

TASK 3 Listen, say the sounds, write **pill, hill**

a. You're going to write the word (pause) **pill.** When you write the word **pill,** you write these sounds: **p** (pause) **iii** (pause) **lll** (pause) **lll.**
b. Say the sounds you write for (pause) **pill.** Get ready. Clap for each sound as the children say *p* (pause) *iii* (pause) *lll* (pause) *lll.* Repeat until firm.
c. Everybody, write the word (pause) **pill.** Check work.
d. Repeat *a* through *c* for **hill.**

TASK 4 Write **wish, barn, red, to, ring, has**

a. You're going to write the word (pause) **wish.** Think about the sounds in **wish** and write the word. Check work.
b. Repeat *a* for **barn, red, to, ring,** and **has.**

SENTENCE WRITING

TASK 5 Write two sentences

a. Listen to this sentence.
   She will hop and sing.
   Say that sentence. Get ready. (Signal.)
   She will hop and sing.
b. Now you're going to say that sentence the slow way. Get ready. (Signal.) Signal for each word as the children say, *She* (pause) *will* (pause) *hop* (pause) *and* (pause) *sing.*
c. Everybody, write the sentence. Spell each word the right way. Check work.
d. Repeat *a* through *c* for **A bug was on a rug.**

LESSON 41

WORD WRITING

TASK 1 Say the sounds, write **cup, us, come, swim, bed, get**

a. You're going to write the word (pause) **cup**. Say the sounds in **cup**. Get ready. Clap for each sound as the children say c (pause) *uuu* (pause) *p*. Repeat until firm.
b. Everybody, write the word (pause) **cup**. Check work.
c. Repeat *a* and *b* for **us, come, swim, bed,** and **get**.

TASK 2 Write **dish, with, hill, arm**

a. You're going to write the word (pause) **dish**. Think about the sounds in **dish** and write the word. Check work.
b. Repeat *a* for **with, hill,** and **arm**.

SENTENCE WRITING

TASK 3 Write two sentences

a. Listen to this sentence.
   The cat was in the car.
   Say that sentence. Get ready. (Signal.)
   The cat was in the car.
b. Now you're going to say that sentence the slow way. Get ready. (Signal.) Signal for each word as the children say, *The* (pause *cat* (pause) *was* (pause) *in* (pause) *the* (pause) *car.*
c. Everybody, write the sentence. Spell each word the right way. Check work.
d. Repeat *a* through *c* for **That fan is not wet.**

LESSON 42

WORD WRITING

TASK 1 Say the sounds, write **us, bus, top, stop, fed**

a. You're going to write the word (pause) **us**. Say the sounds in **us**. Get ready. Clap for each sound as the children say *uuu* (pause) *sss*. Repeat until firm.
b. Everybody, write the word (pause) **us**. Check work.
c. Repeat *a* and *b* for **bus, top, stop,** and **fed**.

TASK 2 Write **bed, swim, if, come, wish, me, has**

a. You're going to write the word (pause) **bed**. Think about the sounds in **bed** and write the word. Check work.
b. Repeat *a* for **swim, if, come, wish, me,** and **has**.

SENTENCE WRITING

TASK 3 Write two sentences

a. Listen to this sentence.
   The rat was on the ship.
   Say that sentence. Get ready. (Signal.)
   The rat was on the ship.
b. Now you're going to say that sentence the slow way. Get ready. (Signal.) Signal for each word as the children say, *The* (pause) *rat* (pause) *was* (pause) *on* (pause) *the* (pause) *ship.*
c. Everybody, write the sentence. Spell each word the right way. Check work.
d. Repeat *a* through *c* for **A dog will run and bark.**

LESSON 43

WORD WRITING

TASK 1 Say the sounds, write **big, pit, ring, sing, dark**

a. You're going to write the word (pause) **big**. Say the sounds in **big**. Get ready. Clap for each sound as the children say *b* (pause) *iii* (pause) *g*. Repeat until firm.
b. Everybody, write the word (pause) **big**. Check work.
c. Repeat *a* and *b* for **pit, ring, sing,** and **dark**.

TASK 2 Write **mop, cop, us, fed, them**

a. You're going to write the word (pause) **mop**. Think about the sounds in **mop** and write the word. Check work.
b. Repeat *a* for **cop, us, fed,** and **them**.

SENTENCE WRITING

TASK 3 Write two sentences

a. Listen to this sentence.
   This fish will swim.
   Say that sentence. Get ready. (Signal.)
   This fish will swim.
b. Now you're going to say that sentence the slow way. Get ready. (Signal.) Signal for each word as the children say, *This* (pause) *fish* (pause) *will* (pause) *swim.*
c. Everybody, write the sentence. Spell each word the right way. Check work.
d. Repeat *a* through *c* for **She did not hit me.**

LESSON 44

WORD WRITING

TASK 1   Listen, say the sounds, write **said**

a. You're going to write the word (pause) **said**. When you write the word **said**, you write these sounds: **sss** (pause) **aaa** (pause) **iii** (pause) **d**.

b. Say the sounds you write for (pause) **said**. Get ready. Clap for each sound as the children say *sss* (pause) *aaa* (pause) *iii* (pause) *d*. Repeat until firm.

c. Everybody, write the word (pause) **said**. Check work.

TASK 2   Say the sounds, write **come, him, then, went, to**

a. You're going to write the word (pause) **come**. Say the sounds in **come**. Get ready. Clap for each sound as the children say *c* (pause) *ooo* (pause) *mmm* (pause) *ēēē*. Repeat until firm.

b. Everybody, write the word (pause) **come**. Check work.

c. Repeat *a* and *b* for **him, then, went,** and **to**.

TASK 3   Write **has, thing, with, get, us, hop**

a. You're going to write the word (pause) **has**. Think about the sounds in **has** and write the word. Check work.

b. Repeat *a* for **thing, with, get, us,** and **hop**.

SENTENCE WRITING

TASK 4   Write two sentences

a. Listen to this sentence. **That man did not run**. Say that sentence. Get ready. (Signal.) *That man did not run.*

b. Now you're going to say that sentence the slow way. Get ready. (Signal.) Signal for each word as the children say, *That* (pause) *man* (pause) *did* (pause) *not* (pause) *run*.

c. Everybody, write the sentence. Spell each word the right way. Check work.

d. Repeat *a* through *c* for **This park is not big.**

LESSON 45

WORD WRITING

TASK 1   Listen, say the sounds, write **said, bell, fell, tell**

a. You're going to write the word (pause) **said**. When you write the word **said**, you write these sounds: **sss** (pause) **aaa** (pause) **iii** (pause) **d**.

b. Say the sounds you write for (pause) **said**. Get ready. Clap for each sound as the children say *sss* (pause) *aaa* (pause) *iii* (pause) *d*. Repeat until firm.

c. Everybody, write the word (pause) **said**. Check work.

d. Repeat *a* through *c* for **bell, fell,** and **tell**.

TASK 2   Say the sounds, write **come, tar, if**

a. You're going to write the word (pause) **come**. Say the sounds in **come**. Get ready. Clap for each sound as the children say *c* (pause) *ooo* (pause) *mmm* (pause) *ēēē*. Repeat until firm.

b. Everybody, write the word (pause) **come**. Check work.

c. Repeat *a* and *b* for **tar** and **if**.

TASK 3   Write **us, bus, with, hill, ring**

a. You're going to write the word (pause) **us**. Think about the sounds in **us** and write the word. Check work.

b. Repeat *a* for **bus, with, hill,** and **ring**.

SENTENCE WRITING

TASK 4   Write two sentences

a. Listen to this sentence. **That cow did not sing**. Say that sentence. Get ready. (Signal.) *That cow did not sing.*

b. Now you're going to say that sentence the slow way. Get ready. (Signal.) Signal for each word as the children say, *That* (pause) *cow* (pause) *did* (pause) *not* (pause) *sing*.

c. Everybody, write the sentence. Spell each word the right way. Check work.

d. Repeat *a* through *c* for **This bug will run and hop.**

LESSON 46

WORD WRITING

TASK 1 Say the sounds, write **sell**, **tell**, **bell**, **said**

a. You're going to write the word (pause) **sell**. Say the sounds in **sell**. Get ready. Clap for each sound as the children say *sss* (pause) *eee* (pause) *lll* (pause) *lll*. Repeat until firm.
b. Everybody, write the word (pause) **sell**. Check work.
c. Repeat a and b for **tell**, **bell**, and **said**.

TASK 2 Write **bet**, **ten**, **bug**, **mud**, **now**, **hit**, **swim**

a. You're going to write the word (pause) **bet**. Think about the sounds in **bet** and write the word. Check work.
b. Repeat a for **ten**, **bug**, **mud**, **now**, **hit**, and **swim**.

SENTENCE WRITING

TASK 3 Write two sentences

a. Listen to this sentence.
We went to the farm.
Say that sentence. Get ready. (Signal.) *We went to the farm*.
b. Now you're going to say that sentence the slow way. Get ready. (Signal.) Signal for each word as the children say, *We* (pause) *went* (pause) *to* (pause) *the* (pause) *farm*.
c. Everybody, write the sentence. Spell each word the right way. Check work.
d. Repeat a through c for **She will come with me**.

LESSON 47

WORD WRITING

TASK 1 Say the sounds, write **bell**, **fell**, **sell**, **thing**, **me**, **she**

a. You're going to write the word (pause) **bell**. Say the sounds in **bell**. Get ready. Clap for each sound as the children say *b* (pause) *eee* (pause) *lll* (pause) *lll*. Repeat until firm.
b. Everybody, write the word (pause) **bell**. Check work.
c. Repeat a and b for **fell**, **sell**, **thing**, **me**, and **she**.

TASK 2 Write **do**, **said**, **them**, **come**, **hill**, **mad**

a. You're going to write the word (pause) **do**. Think about the sounds in **do** and write the word. Check work.
b. Repeat a for **said**, **them**, **come**, **hill**, and **mad**.

SENTENCE WRITING

TASK 3 Write two sentences

a. Listen to this sentence.
The dog went to the barn.
Say that sentence. Get ready. (Signal.) *The dog went to the barn*.
b. Now you're going to say that sentence the slow way. Get ready. (Signal.) Signal for each word as the children say, *The* (pause) *dog* (pause) *went* (pause) *to* (pause) *the* (pause) *barn*.
c. Everybody, write the sentence. Spell each word the right way. Check work.
d. Repeat a through c for **A cow will run with us**.

LESSON 48

WORD WRITING

TASK 1 Say the sounds, write **dish**, **wish**, **fish**, **if**, **bark**, **sand**

a. You're going to write the word (pause) **dish**. Say the sounds in **dish**. Get ready. Clap for each sound as the children say *d* (pause) *iii* (pause) *sh*. Repeat until firm.
b. Everybody, write the word (pause) **dish**. Check work.
c. Repeat a and b for **wish**, **fish**, **if**, **bark**, and **sand**.

TASK 2 Write **well**, **tell**, **said**, **his**, **has**

a. You're going to write the word (pause) **well**. Think about the sounds in **well** and write the word. Check work.
b. Repeat a for **tell**, **said**, **his**, and **has**.

SENTENCE WRITING

TASK 3 Write two sentences

a. Listen to this sentence.
He will come with us.
Say that sentence. Get ready. (Signal.) *He will come with us*.
b. Now you're going to say that sentence the slow way. Get ready. (Signal.) Signal for each word as the children say, *He* (pause) *will* (pause) *come* (pause) *with* (pause) *us*.
c. Everybody, write the sentence. Spell each word the right way. Check work.
d. Repeat a through c for **That cop was mad**.

LESSON 49

WORD WRITING

TASK 1 Say the sounds, write **cup**, **up**, **us**, **bell**, **ship**, **cow**

a. You're going to write the word (pause) **cup**. Say the sounds in **cup**. Get ready.
   Clap for each sound as the children say *c* (pause) *uuu* (pause) *p*. Repeat until firm.
b. Everybody, write the word (pause) **cup**. Check work.
c. Repeat *a* and *b* for **up**, **us**, **bell**, **ship**, and **cow**.

TASK 2 Write **to**, **went**, **car**, **fell**, **sing**, **how**

a. You're going to write the word (pause) **to**. Think about the sounds in **to** and write the word. Check work.
b. Repeat *a* for **went**, **car**, **fell**, **sing**, and **how**.

SENTENCE WRITING

TASK 3 Write two sentences

a. Listen to this sentence.
   That dish was in the mud.
   Say that sentence. Get ready. (Signal.)
   That dish was in the mud.
b. Now you're going to say that sentence the slow way. Get ready. (Signal.) Signal for each word as the children say, *That* (pause) *dish* (pause) *was* (pause) *in* (pause) *the* (pause) *mud.*
c. Everybody, write the sentence. Spell each word the right way. Check work.
d. Repeat *a* through *c* for **His dog will bark.**

LESSON 50

SOUND WRITING

TASK 1 Introduce sound combination **al**

a. Write on the board: **al**.
b. Point to **al**. Everybody, tell me the sound these letters make. Get ready. (Signal.) *All.* Yes, **all**.
c. Erase **al**. Everybody, write the two letters that go together and make the sound **all**. Check work.

WORD WRITING

TASK 2 Say the sounds, write **swim**, **ring**, **wet**, **hand**

a. You're going to write the word (pause) **swim**. Say the sounds in **swim**. Get ready.
   Clap for each sound as the children say *sss* (pause) *www* (pause) *iii* (pause) *mmm*. Repeat until firm.
b. Everybody, write the word (pause) **swim**. Check work.
c. Repeat *a* and *b* for **ring**, **wet**, and **hand**.

TASK 3 Write **sand**, **it**, **hill**, **well**, **met**, **said**

a. You're going to write the word (pause) **sand**. Think about the sounds in **sand** and write the word. Check work.
b. Repeat *a* for **it**, **hill**, **well**, **met**, and **said**.

SENTENCE WRITING

TASK 4 Write two sentences

a. Listen to this sentence.
   The hen sat on the fan.
   Say that sentence. Get ready. (Signal.)
   The hen sat on the fan.
b. Now you're going to say that sentence the slow way. Get ready. (Signal.) Signal for each word as the children say, *The* (pause) *hen* (pause) *sat* (pause) *on* (pause) *the* (pause) *fan.*
c. Everybody, write the sentence. Spell each word the right way. Check work.
d. Repeat *a* through *c* for **His cat ran in the park.**

LESSON 51

SOUND WRITING

TASK 1 Introduce sound combination **al**

a. Write on the board: **al**.
b. Point to **al**. Everybody, tell me the sound these letters make. Get ready. (Signal.) *All.* Yes, **all**.
c. Erase **al**. Everybody, write the two letters that go together and make the sound **all**. Check work.

WORD WRITING

TASK 2 Write sound combination words **all, ball, fall, also**

a. Write on the board: **all, ball, fall, also.**
b. Point to **all.** Everybody, read this word the fast way. Get ready. (Signal.) *All.* Yes, **all.**
c. Everybody, say the sounds you write for the word (pause) **all.** Get ready. Touch **al, l** as the children say *al* (pause) *lll.* Repeat until firm.
d. Erase **all.** Everybody, write the word (pause) **all.** Check work.
e. Repeat *b* through *d* for **ball, fall,** and **also.**

TASK 3 Say the sounds, write **cap, pig, nut**

a. You're going to write the word (pause) **cap.** Say the sounds in **cap.** Get ready. Clap for each sound as the children say *c* (pause) *aaa* (pause) *p.* Repeat until firm.
b. Everybody, write the word (pause) **cap.** Check work.
c. Repeat *a* and *b* for **pig** and **nut.**

TASK 4 Write **big, rug, bus, dark**

a. You're going to write the word (pause) **big.** Think about the sounds in **big** and write the word. Check work.
b. Repeat *a* for **rug, bus,** and **dark.**

SENTENCE WRITING

TASK 5 Write two sentences

a. Listen to this sentence. **His dog can swim.** Say that sentence. Get ready. (Signal.) *His dog can swim.*
b. Now you're going to say that sentence the slow way. Get ready. (Signal.) Signal for each word as the children say, *His* (pause) *dog* (pause) *can* (pause) *swim.*
c. Everybody, write the sentence. Spell each word the right way. Check work.
d. Repeat *a* through *c* for **She will sell a hat.**

LESSON 52

SOUND WRITING

TASK 1 Introduce sound combination **al**

a. Write on the board: **al.**
b. Point to **al.** Everybody, tell me the sound these letters make. Get ready. (Signal.) *All.* Yes, **all.**
c. Erase **al.** Everybody, write the two letters that go together and make the sound **all.** Check work.

WORD WRITING

TASK 2 Write sound combination words **salt, call, fall**

a. Write on the board: **salt, call, fall.**
b. Point to **salt.** Everybody, read this word the fast way. Get ready. (Signal.) *Salt.* Yes, **salt.**
c. Everybody, say the sounds you write for the word (pause) **salt.** Get ready. Touch **s, al, t** as the children say *sss* (pause) *al* (pause) *t.* Repeat until firm.
d. Erase **salt.** Everybody, write the word (pause) **salt.** Check work.
e. Repeat *b* through *d* for **call** and **fall.**

TASK 3 Say the sounds, write **come, bark**

a. You're going to write the word (pause) **come.** Say the sounds in **come.** Get ready. Clap for each sound as the children say *c* (pause) *ooo* (pause) *mmm* (pause) *ēēē.* Repeat until firm.
b. Everybody, write the word (pause) **come.** Check work.
c. Repeat *a* and *b* for **bark.**

TASK 4 Write **sand, hand, bet, said, has, bug**

a. You're going to write the word (pause) **sand.** Think about the sounds in **sand** and write the word. Check work.
b. Repeat *a* for **hand, bet, said, has,** and **bug.**

SENTENCE WRITING

TASK 5   Write two sentences

a. Listen to this sentence.
His pig went with him.
Say that sentence. Get ready. (Signal.)
His pig went with him.

b. Now you're going to say that sentence the
slow way. Get ready. (Signal.) Signal for
each word as the children say, *His* (pause)
pig (pause) *went* (pause) *with* (pause) *him.*

c. Everybody, write the sentence. Spell each
word the right way. Check work.

d. Repeat *a* through *c* for **His cap is in the mud.**

LESSON 53

SOUND WRITING

TASK 1   Write al

a. Everybody, you're going to write the two
letters that go together and make the
sound **all**. What sound? (Signal.) *All.*

b. Write **all.** Check work.

WORD WRITING

TASK 2   Write sound combination words
also, call, ball

a. Write on the board: **also, call, ball.**

b. Point to **also.** Everybody, read this word
the fast way. Get ready. (Signal.) *Also.*
Yes, **also.**

c. Everybody, say the sounds you write for
the word (pause) **also.** Get ready. Touch
al, s, o as the children say *al* (pause) *sss*
(pause) *ōōō.* Repeat until firm.

d. Erase **also.** Everybody, write the word
(pause) **also.** Check work.

e. Repeat *b* through *d* for **call** and **ball.**

TASK 3   Say the sounds, write **how, wish,
it, hit, shop, met, hand**

a. You're going to write the word (pause)
how. Say the sounds in **how.** Get ready.
Clap for each sound as the children say
h (pause) *ooo* (pause) *www.* Repeat until
firm.

b. Everybody, write the word (pause) **how.**
Check work.

c. Repeat *a* and *b* for **wish, it, hit, shop, met,**
and **hand.**

TASK 4   Write **do, if**

a. You're going to write the word (pause)
do. Think about the sounds in **do** and write
the word. Check work.

b. Repeat *a* for **if.**

SENTENCE WRITING

TASK 5   Write two sentences

a. Listen to this sentence.
She will sell a bell.
Say that sentence. Get ready. (Signal.)
She will sell a bell.

b. Now you're going to say that sentence the
slow way. Get ready. (Signal.) Signal for
each word as the children say, *She* (pause)
will (pause) *sell* (pause) *a* (pause) *bell.*

c. Everybody, write the sentence. Spell each
word the right way. Check work.

d. Repeat *a* through *c* for **The nut was not fat.**

LESSON 54

SOUND WRITING

TASK 1   Write al

a. Everybody, you're going to write the two
letters that go together and make the
sound **all**. What sound? (Signal.) *All.*

b. Write **all.** Check work.

WORD WRITING

TASK 2   Write sound combination words
tall, salt, wall

a. Write on the board: **tall, salt, wall.**

b. Point to **tall.** Everybody, read this
word the fast way. Get ready. (Signal.)
Tall. Yes, **tall.**

c. Everybody, say the sounds you write for
the word (pause) **tall.** Get ready. Touch
t, al, l as the children say *t* (pause) *al*
(pause) *lll.* Repeat until firm.

d. Erase **tall.** Everybody, write the word
(pause) **tall.** Check work.

e. Repeat *b* through *d* for **salt** and **wall.**

TASK 3 Say the sounds, write **fell**, **card**, **rug**

a. You're going to write the word (pause) **fell**. Say the sounds in **fell**. Get ready. Clap for each sound as the children say *fff* (pause) *eee* (pause) *lll* (pause) *lll*. Repeat until firm.

b. Everybody, write the word (pause) **fell**. Check work.

c. Repeat *a* and *b* for **card** and **rug**.

TASK 4 Write **did**, **big**, **cap**, **his**, **now**

a. You're going to write the word (pause) **did**. Think about the sounds in **did** and write the word. Check work.

b. Repeat *a* for **big**, **cap**, **his**, and **now**.

SENTENCE WRITING

TASK 5 Write two sentences

a. Listen to this sentence. **The dog will sing with us**. Say that sentence. Get ready. (Signal.) *The dog will sing with us.*

b. Now you're going to say that sentence the slow way. Get ready. (Signal.) Signal for each word as the children say, *The* (pause) *dog* (pause) *will* (pause) *sing* (pause) *with* (pause) *us.*

c. Everybody, write the sentence. Spell each word the right way. Check work.

d. Repeat *a* through *c* for **She is on the bus.**

LESSON 55

WORD WRITING

TASK 1 Say the sounds, write **tall**, **wall**, **wish**, **said**, **tap**

a. You're going to write the word (pause) **tall**. Say the sounds in **tall**. Get ready. Clap for each sound as the children say *t* (pause) *al* (pause) *lll*. Repeat until firm.

b. Everybody, write the word (pause) **tall**. Check work.

c. Repeat *a* and *b* for **wall**, **wish**, **said**, and **tap**.

TASK 2 Write **them**, **tell**, **card**, **to**, **ship**, **cap**

a. You're going to write the word (pause) **them**. Think about the sounds in **them** and write the word. Check work.

b. Repeat *a* for **tell**, **card**, **to**, **ship**, and **cap**.

SENTENCE WRITING

TASK 3 Write two sentences

a. Listen to this sentence. **We will hop and sing**. Say that sentence. Get ready. (Signal.) *We will hop and sing.*

b. Now you're going to say that sentence the slow way. Get ready. (Signal.) Signal for each word as the children say, *We* (pause) *will* (pause) *hop* (pause) *and* (pause) *sing.*

c. Everybody, write the sentence. Spell each word the right way. Check work.

d. Repeat *a* through *c* for **She did not hit me.**

LESSON 56

SOUND WRITING

TASK 1 Write **sh**, **ar**, **th**, **al**, **ing**

a. Everybody, you're going to write the letters that go together and make the sound **sh**. What sound? (Signal.) *sh.*

b. Write **sh**. Check work.

c. Repeat *a* and *b* for **ar**, **th**, **al**, and **ing**.

WORD WRITING

TASK 2 Say the sounds, write **salt**, **card**, **now**, **swim**, **this**

a. You're going to write the word (pause) **salt**. Say the sounds in **salt**. Get ready. Clap for each sound as the children say *sss* (pause) *al* (pause) *t*. Repeat until firm.

b. Everybody, write the word (pause) **salt**. Check work.

c. Repeat *a* and *b* for **card**, **now**, **swim**, and **this**.

TASK 3 Write **call**, **fun**, **get**, **ring**, **ham**

a. You're going to write the word (pause) **call**. Think about the sounds in **call** and write the word. Check work.

b. Repeat *a* for **fun**, **get**, **ring**, and **ham**.

SENTENCE WRITING

TASK 4   Write two sentences

a. Listen to this sentence.
   That bell did not ring.
   Say that sentence. Get ready.   (Signal.)
   That bell did not ring.
b. Now you're going to say that sentence the
   slow way. Get ready.   (Signal.) Signal for
   each word as the children say, *That* (pause)
   bell (pause) *did* (pause) *not* (pause) *ring.*
c. Everybody, write the sentence. Spell each
   word the right way.   Check work.
d. Repeat *a* through *c* for **He can run with us.**

LESSON 57

SOUND WRITING

TASK 1   Write **sh, th, ar, al, ing**

a. Everybody, you're going to write the
   letters that go together and make the
   sound **sh**. What sound?   (Signal.) *sh.*
b. Write **sh**.   Check work.
c. Repeat *a* and *b* for **th, ar, al,** and **ing.**

WORD WRITING

TASK 2   Listen, say the sounds, write **of, stop**

a. You're going to write the word   (pause)
   of. When you write the word **of**, you write
   these sounds: *ooo*   (pause) *fff*.
b. Say the sounds you write for   (pause) **of**.
   Get ready.   Clap for each sound as the
   children say *ooo* (pause) *fff*. Repeat until
   firm.

c. Everybody, write the word   (pause) **of**.
   Check work.
d. Repeat *a* through *c* for **stop.**

TASK 3   Say the sounds, write **to, also, went**

a. You're going to write the word   (pause) **to**.
   Say the sounds in **to**. Get ready.   Clap for
   each sound as the children say *t* (pause)
   ooo.   Repeat until firm.
b. Everybody, write the word   (pause) **to**.
   Check work.
c. Repeat *a* and *b* for **also** and **went.**

TASK 4   Write **fish, him, wall, hand, thing**

a. You're going to write the word   (pause)
   fish.   Think about the sounds in **fish** and
   write the word.   Check work.
b. Repeat *a* for **him, wall, hand,** and **thing.**

SENTENCE WRITING

TASK 5   Write two sentences

a. Listen to this sentence.
   His card is red.
   Say that sentence. Get ready.   (Signal.)
   His card is red.
b. Now you're going to say that sentence the
   slow way. Get ready.   (Signal.) Signal for
   each word as the children say, *His* (pause)
   card (pause) *is* (pause) *red.*
c. Everybody, write the sentence. Spell each
   word the right way.   Check work.
d. Repeat *a* through *c* for **This cat has a bell.**

LESSON 58

SOUND WRITING

TASK 1   Write **th, sh, ar, ing, al**

a. Everybody, you're going to write the
   letters that go together and make the
   sound **th**. What sound?   (Signal.) *th.*
b. Write **th**.   Check work.
c. Repeat *a* and *b* for **sh, ar, ing,** and **al.**

WORD WRITING

TASK 2   Say the sounds, write **said, cup, of, stop**

a. You're going to write the word   (pause)
   said. Say the sounds in **said**. Get ready.
   Clap for each sound as the children say
   sss (pause) *aaa* (pause) *iii* (pause) *d*. Repeat
   until firm.
b. Everybody, write the word   (pause) **said**.
   Check work.
c. Repeat *a* and *b* for **cup, of,** and **stop.**

TASK 3   Write **shop, if, big, fall, wet, met, us**

a. You're going to write the word   (pause)
   shop. Think about the sounds in **shop**
   and write the word.   Check work.
b. Repeat *a* for **if, big, fall, wet, met,** and **us.**

SENTENCE WRITING

TASK 4 Write two sentences

a. Listen to this sentence. **We will sit and sing.** Say that sentence. Get ready. (Signal.) *We will sit and sing.*

b. Now you're going to say that sentence the slow way. Get ready. (Signal.) Signal for each word as the children say, *We* (pause) *will* (pause) *sit* (pause) *and* (pause) *sing.*

c. Everybody, write the sentence. Spell each word the right way. Check work.

d. Repeat *a* through *c* for **That cow did not bark.**

LESSON 59

SOUND WRITING

TASK 1 Introduce sound combination wh

a. Write on the board: **wh.**

b. Point to **wh.** Everybody, tell me the sound these letters make. Get ready. (Signal.) *wh.* Yes, **wh.**

c. Erase **wh.** Everybody, write the letters that go together and make the sound **wh.** Check work.

WORD WRITING

TASK 2 Say the sounds, write sing, sand, arm, salt, swim

a. You're going to write the word (pause) **sing.** Say the sounds in **sing.** Get ready. Clap for each sound as the children say *sss* (pause) *ing.* Repeat until firm.

b. Everybody, write the word (pause) **sing.** Check work.

c. Repeat *a* and *b* for **sand, arm, salt,** and **swim.**

TASK 3 Write cap, bed, fish, of, stop

a. You're going to write the word (pause) **cap.** Think about the sounds in **cap** and write the word. Check work.

b. Repeat *a* for **bed, fish, of,** and **stop.**

SENTENCE WRITING

TASK 4 Write two sentences

a. Listen to this sentence. **He will run and fall.** Say that sentence. Get ready. (Signal.) *He will run and fall.*

b. Now you're going to say that sentence the slow way. Get ready. (Signal.) Signal for each word as the children say, *He* (pause) *will* (pause) *run* (pause) *and* (pause) *fall.*

c. Everybody, write the sentence. Spell each word the right way. Check work.

d. Repeat *a* through *c* for **A ball fell in the mud.**

LESSON 60

SOUND WRITING

TASK 1 Introduce sound combination wh

a. Write on the board: **wh.**

b. Point to **wh.** Everybody, tell me the sound these letters make. Get ready. (Signal.) *wh.* Yes, **wh.**

c. Erase **wh.** Everybody, write the letters that go together and make the sound **wh.** Check work.

WORD WRITING

TASK 2 Write sound combination words where, when, what

a. Write on the board: **where, when, what.**

b. Point to **where.** Everybody, read this word the fast way. Get ready. (Signal.) *Where.* Yes, **where.**

c. Everybody, say the sounds you write for the word (pause) **where.** Get ready. Touch **wh, e, r, e** as the children say *wh* (pause) *eee* (pause) *rrr* (pause) *ēēē.* Repeat until firm.

d. Erase **where.** Everybody, write the word (pause) **where.** Check work.

e. Repeat *b* through *d* for **when** and **what.**

TASK 3 Say the sounds, write **him**, **with**, **pill**

a. You're going to write the word (pause) **him**. Say the sounds in **him**. Get ready. Clap for each sound as the children say *h* (pause) *iii* (pause) *mmm*. Repeat until firm.
b. Everybody, write the word (pause) **him**. Check work.
c. Repeat *a* and *b* for **with** and **pill**.

TASK 4 Write **fed**, **red**, **car**, **stop**, **also**

a. You're going to write the word (pause) **fed**. Think about the sounds in **fed** and write the word. Check work.
b. Repeat *a* for **red, car, stop**, and **also**.

SENTENCE WRITING

TASK 5 Write two sentences

a. Listen to this sentence.
   His cap fell in the sand.
   Say that sentence. Get ready. (Signal.) *His cap fell in the sand.*
b. Now you're going to say that sentence the slow way. Get ready. (Signal.) Signal for each word as the children say, *His* (pause) *cap* (pause) *fell* (pause) *in* (pause) *the* (pause) *sand.*
c. Everybody, write the sentence. Spell each word the right way. Check work.
d. Repeat *a* through *c* for **This pig can run.**

LESSON 61

SOUND WRITING

TASK 1 Introduce sound combination **wh**

a. Write on the board: **wh**.
b. Point to **wh**. Everybody, tell me the sound these letters make. Get ready. (Signal.) *wh.* Yes, **wh**.
c. Erase **wh**. Everybody, write the letters that go together and make the sound **wh**. Check work.

WORD WRITING

TASK 2 Write sound combination words **when, where, what**

a. Write on the board: **when, where, what**.
b. Point to **when**. Everybody, read this word the fast way. Get ready. (Signal.) *When.* Yes, **when**.
c. Everybody, say the sounds you write for the word(pause) **when**. Get ready. Touch **wh, e, n** as the children say *wh* (pause) *eee* (pause) *nnn*. Repeat until firm.
d. Erase **when**. Everybody, write the word (pause) **when**. Check work.
e. Repeat *b* through *d* for **where** and **what**.

TASK 3 Say the sounds, write **thing**, **now**, **dish**

a. You're going to write the word (pause) **thing**. Say the sounds in **thing**. Get ready. Clap for each sound as the children say *th* (pause) *ing*. Repeat until firm.
b. Everybody, write the word (pause) **thing**. Check work.
c. Repeat *a* and *b* for **now** and **dish**.

TASK 4 Write **ten**, **sand**, **of**, **hen**, **bug**, **salt**

a. You're going to write the word (pause) **ten**. Think about the sounds in **ten** and write the word. Check work.
b. Repeat *a* for **sand, of, hen, bug**, and **salt**.

SENTENCE WRITING

TASK 5 Write two sentences

a. Listen to this sentence.
   The mop is on the rug.
   Say that sentence. Get ready. (Signal.) *The mop is on the rug.*
b. Now you're going to say that sentence the slow way. Get ready. (Signal.) Signal for each word as the children say, *The* (pause) *mop* (pause) *is* (pause) *on* (pause) *the* (pause) *rug.*
c. Everybody, write the sentence. Spell each word the right way. Check work.
d. Repeat *a* through *c* for **His dog has a bell.**

LESSON 62

SOUND WRITING

TASK 1   Write wh

a. Everybody, you're going to write the letters that go together and make the sound **wh**. What sound?   (Signal.) *wh*.
b. Write **wh**.   Check work.

WORD WRITING

TASK 2   Write sound combination words when, what, where

a. Write on the board: **when, what, where**.
b. Point to **when**. Everybody, read this word the fast way. Get ready.   (Signal.) *When*.   Yes, **when**.
c. Everybody, say the sounds you write for the word   (pause) **when**. Get ready.   Touch **wh, e, n** as the children say *wh* (pause) *eee* (pause) *nnn*. Repeat until firm.
d. Erase **when**. Everybody, write the word (pause) **when**.   Check work.
e. Repeat *b* through *d* for **what** and **where**.

TASK 3   Say the sounds, write wish, hut, come, said

a. You're going to write the word   (pause) **wish**. Say the sounds in **wish**. Get ready.   Clap for each sound as the children say *www* (pause) *iii* (pause) *sh*. Repeat until firm.
b. Everybody, write the word   (pause) **wish**. Check work.
c. Repeat *a* and *b* for **hut, come**, and **said**.

TASK 4   Write bark, to, but, hill

a. You're going to write the word   (pause) **bark**. Think about the sounds in **bark** and write the word.   Check work.
b. Repeat *a* for **to, but**, and **hill**.

SENTENCE WRITING

TASK 5   Write two sentences

a. Listen to this sentence. **His pig can sing**. Say that sentence. Get ready.   (Signal.) *His pig can sing.*
b. Now you're going to say that sentence the slow way. Get ready.   (Signal.) Signal for each word as the children say, *His* (pause) *pig* (pause) *can* (pause) *sing.*
c. Everybody, write the sentence. Spell each word the right way.   Check work.
d. Repeat *a* through *c* for **That hen is not tall.**

LESSON 63

SOUND WRITING

TASK 1   Write wh

a. Everybody, you're going to write the letters that go together and make the sound **wh**. What sound?   (Signal.) *wh*.
b. Write **wh**.   Check work.

WORD WRITING

TASK 2   Write sound combination words what, where, when

a. Write on the board: **what, where, when**.
b. Point to **what**. Everybody, read this word the fast way. Get ready.   (Signal.) *What.* Yes, **what.**
c. Everybody, say the sounds you write for the word   (pause) **what**. Get ready.   Touch **wh, a, t** as the children say *wh* (pause) *aaa* (pause) *t*. Repeat until firm.
d. Erase **what**. Everybody, write the word (pause) **what**.   Check work.
e. Repeat *b* through *d* for **where** and **when**.

TASK 3   Listen, say the sounds, write are

a. You're going to write the word   (pause) **are**. When you write the word **are**, you write these sounds: **ar**   (pause) $\overline{ee}\overline{e}$.
b. Say the sounds you write for   (pause) **are**. Get ready.   Clap for each sound as the children say *ar* (pause) *ēēē*. Repeat until firm.
c. Everybody, write the word   (pause) **are**. Check work.

TASK 4   Say the sounds, write stop, if, ball

a. You're going to write the word   (pause) **stop**. Say the sounds in **stop**. Get ready.   Clap for each sound as the children say *sss* (pause) *t* (pause) *ooo* (pause) *p*. Repeat until firm.
b. Everybody, write the word   (pause) **stop**. Check work.
c. Repeat *a* and *b* for **if** and **ball**.

TASK 5 Write **tall, cow, us, bus**

a. You're going to write the word (pause) **tall**. Think about the sounds in **tall** and write the word. Check work.

b. Repeat *a* for **cow, us,** and **bus.**

SENTENCE WRITING

TASK 6 Write two sentences

a. Listen to this sentence.
She will sit with me.
Say that sentence. Get ready. (Signal.)
She will sit with me.

b. Now you're going to say that sentence the slow way. Get ready. (Signal.) Signal for each word as the children say, *She* (pause) *will* (pause) *sit* (pause) *with* (pause) *me.*

c. Everybody, write the sentence. Spell each word the right way. Check work.

d. Repeat *a* through *c* for **That hen is in the sun.**

LESSON 64

WORD WRITING

TASK 1 Listen, say the sounds, write **are**

a. You're going to write the word (pause) **are**. When you write the word **are**, you write these sounds: *ar* (pause) $\overline{eee}$.

b. Say the sounds you write for (pause) **are**. Get ready. Clap for each sound as the children say *ar* (pause) $\overline{eee}$. Repeat until firm.

c. Everybody, write the word (pause) **are**. Check work.

TASK 2 Say the sounds, write **barn, stop, went, what, where**

a. You're going to write the word (pause) **barn**. Say the sounds in **barn**. Get ready. Clap for each sound as the children say *b* (pause) *ar* (pause) *nnn*. Repeat until firm.

b. Everybody, write the word (pause) **barn**. Check work.

c. Repeat *a* and *b* for **stop, went, what,** and **where.**

TASK 3 Write **far, hill, ship, cop, ring**

a. You're going to write the word (pause) **far**. Think about the sounds in **far** and write the word. Check work.

b. Repeat *a* for **hill, ship, cop,** and **ring.**

SENTENCE WRITING

TASK 4 Write two sentences

a. Listen to this sentence.
This ball is big.
Say that sentence. Get ready. (Signal.)
This ball is big.

b. Now you're going to say that sentence the slow way. Get ready. (Signal.) Signal for each word as the children say, *This* (pause) *ball* (pause) *is* (pause) *big.*

c. Everybody, write the sentence. Spell each word the right way. Check work.

d. Repeat *a* through *c* for **She did not call him.**

LESSON 65

WORD WRITING

TASK 1 Say the sounds, write **are, when, also, where, come**

a. You're going to write the word (pause) **are**. Say the sounds in **are**. Get ready. Clap for each sound as the children say *ar* (pause) $\overline{eee}$. Repeat until firm.

b. Everybody, write the word (pause) **are**. Check work.

c. Repeat *a* and *b* for **when, also, where,** and **come.**

TASK 2 Write **up, cup, sand, ham, met, wall**

a. You're going to write the word (pause) **up**. Think about the sounds in **up** and write the word. Check work.

b. Repeat *a* for **cup, sand, ham, met,** and **wall.**

SENTENCE WRITING

TASK 3 Write two sentences

a. Listen to this sentence.
His bell did not ring.
Say that sentence. Get ready. (Signal.)
His bell did not ring.

b. Now you're going to say that sentence the slow way. Get ready. (Signal.) Signal for each word as the children say, *His* (pause) *bell* (pause) *did* (pause) *not* (pause) *ring.*

c. Everybody, write the sentence. Spell each word the right way. Check work.

d. Repeat *a* through *c* for **This cow has a barn.**

LESSON 66

SOUND WRITING

TASK 1   Introduce sound combination er

a. Write on the board: **er.**
b. Point to **er.** Everybody, tell me the sound these letters make. Get ready. (Signal.) *er.* Yes, **er.**
c. Erase **er.** Everybody, write the letters that go together and make the sound **er.** Check work.

WORD WRITING

TASK 2   Say the sounds, write **stop, dug, salt, swim**

a. You're going to write the word (pause) **stop.** Say the sounds in **stop.** Get ready. Clap for each sound as the children say *sss* (pause) *t* (pause) *ooo* (pause) *p.* Repeat until firm.
b. Everybody, write the word (pause) **stop.** Check work.
c. Repeat a and b for **dug, salt,** and **swim.**

TASK 3   Write **are, cop, shop, what, then, park**

a. You're going to write the word (pause) **are.** Think about the sounds in **are** and write the word. Check work.
b. Repeat a for **cop, shop, what, then,** and **park.**

SENTENCE WRITING

TASK 4   Write two sentences

a. Listen to this sentence. **His dog has the ham.** Say that sentence. Get ready. (Signal.) *His dog has the ham.*
b. Now you're going to say that sentence the slow way. Get ready. (Signal.) Signal for each word as the children say, *His* (pause) *dog* (pause) *has* (pause) *the* (pause) *ham.*
c. Everybody, write the sentence. Spell each word the right way. Check work.
d. Repeat a through c for **The pig ran up the hill.**

LESSON 67

SOUND WRITING

TASK 1   Introduce sound combination er

a. Write on the board: **er.**
b. Point to **er.** Everybody, tell me the sound these letters make. Get ready. (Signal.) *er.* Yes, **er.**
c. Erase **er.** Everybody, write the letters that go together and make the sound **er.** Check work.

WORD WRITING

TASK 2   Write sound combination words **ever, never, other, her**

a. Write on the board: **ever, never, other, her.**
b. Point to **ever.** Everybody, read this word the fast way. Get ready. (Signal.) *Ever.* Yes, **ever.**
c. Everybody, say the sounds you write for the word (pause) **ever.** Get ready. Touch **e, v, er** as the children say *eee* (pause) *vvv* (pause) *er.* Repeat until firm.
d. Erase **ever.** Everybody, write the word (pause) **ever.** Check work.
e. Repeat b through d for **never, other,** and **her.**

TASK 3   Say the sounds, write **how, do, with**

a. You're going to write the word (pause) **how.** Say the sounds in **how.** Get ready. Clap for each sound as the children say *h* (pause) *ooo* (pause) *www.* Repeat until firm.
b. Everybody, write the word (pause) **how.** Check work.
c. Repeat a and b for **do** and **with.**

TASK 4   Write **when, of, tell, fell, big**

a. You're going to write the word (pause) **when.** Think about the sounds in **when** and write the word. Check work.
b. Repeat a for **of, tell, fell,** and **big.**

SENTENCE WRITING

TASK 5   Write two sentences

a. Listen to this sentence.
   The man has the cup.
   Say that sentence. Get ready. (Signal.)
   The man has the cup.
b. Now you're going to say that sentence
   the slow way. Get ready. (Signal.) Signal
   for each word as the children say, *The*
   (pause) *man* (pause) *has* (pause) *the* (pause)
   cup.
c. Everybody, write the sentence. Spell each
   word the right way. Check work.
d. Repeat *a* through *c* for **A cow ran up the
   hill.**

LESSON 68

SOUND WRITING

TASK 1   Introduce sound combination er

a. Write on the board: **er.**
b. Point to **er.** Everybody, tell me the sound
   these letters make. Get ready. (Signal.)
   er. Yes, **er.**
c. Erase **er.** Everybody, write the letters
   that go together and make the sound
   er. Check work.

WORD WRITING

TASK 2   Write sound combination words
her, other, never

a. Write on the board: **her, other, never.**
b. Point to **her.** Everybody, read this word
   the fast way. Get ready. (Signal.) *Her.*
   Yes, **her.**
c. Everybody, say the sounds you write for
   the word (pause) **her.** Get ready. Touch
   h, er as the children say *h* (pause) *er.*
   Repeat until firm.
d. Erase **her.** Everybody, write the word
   (pause) **her.** Check work.
e. Point to **other.** Everybody, read this word
   the fast way. Get ready. (Signal.) *Other.*
   Yes, **other.**
f. Everybody, say the sounds you write for
   the word (pause) **other.** Get ready.
   Touch **o, th, er** as the children say *ooo*
   (pause) *th* (pause) *er.* Repeat until firm.
g. Erase **other.** Everybody, write the word
   (pause) **other.** Check work.
h. Repeat *e* through *g* for **never.**

TASK 3   Say the sounds, write what, sell,
had

a. You're going to write the word (pause)
   what. Say the sounds in **what.** Get ready.
   Clap for each sound as the children say
   wh (pause) *aaa* (pause) *t.* Repeat until firm.
b. Everybody, write the word (pause) **what.**
   Check work.
c. Repeat *a* and *b* for **sell** and **had.**

TASK 4   Write it, hit, fit, top, men, at

a. You're going to write the word (pause)
   it. Think about the sounds in **it** and write
   the word. Check work.
b. Repeat *a* for **hit, fit, top, men,** and **at.**

SENTENCE WRITING

TASK 5   Write two sentences

a. Listen to this sentence.
   That fish will get fat.
   Say that sentence. Get ready. (Signal.)
   That fish will get fat.
b. Now you're going to say that sentence the
   slow way. Get ready. (Signal.) Signal for
   each word as the children say, *That* (pause)
   fish (pause) *will* (pause) *get* (pause) *fat.*
c. Everybody, write the sentence. Spell each
   word the right way. Check work.
d. Repeat *a* through *c* for **His dog can run and
   bark.**

LESSON 69

SOUND WRITING

TASK 1   Write er

a. Everybody, you're going to write the
   letters that go together and make the
   sound **er.** What sound? (Signal.) *er.*
b. Write **er.** Check work.

WORD WRITING

TASK 2 Write sound combination words **never, other, ever, her**

a. Write on the board: **never, other, ever, her.**
b. Point to **never.** Everybody, read this word the fast way. Get ready. (Signal.) *Never.* Yes, **never.**
c. Everybody, say the sounds you write for the word (pause) **never.** Get ready. Touch **n, e, v, er** as the children say *nnn* (pause) *eee* (pause) *vvv* (pause) *er.* Repeat until firm.
d. Erase **never.** Everybody, write the word (pause) **never.** Check work.
e. Repeat *b* through *d* for **other, ever,** and **her.**

TASK 3 Say the sounds, write **pet, shot, got**

a. You're going to write the word (pause) **pet.** Say the sounds in **pet.** Get ready. Clap for each sound as the children say *p* (pause) *eee* (pause) *t.* Repeat until firm.
b. Everybody, write the word (pause) **pet.** Check work.
c. Repeat *a* and *b* for **shot** and **got.**

TASK 4 Write **pit, had, when, farm**

a. You're going to write the word (pause) **pit.** Think about the sounds in **pit** and write the word. Check work.
b. Repeat *a* for **had, when,** and **farm.**

SENTENCE WRITING

TASK 5 Write two sentences

a. Listen to this sentence.
We did not get wet.
Say that sentence. Get ready. (Signal.) *We did not get wet.*
b. Now you're going to say that sentence the slow way. Get ready. (Signal.) Signal for each word as the children say, *We* (pause) *did* (pause) *not* (pause) *get* (pause) *wet.*
c. Everybody, write the sentence. Spell each word the right way. Check work.
d. Repeat *a* through *c* for **She has a dog and a cat.**

LESSON 70

SOUND WRITING

TASK 1 Write **er**

a. Everybody, you're going to write the letters that go together and make the sound **er.** What sound? (Signal.) *er.*
b. Write **er.** Check work.

WORD WRITING

TASK 2 Write sound combination words **ever, other, her, never**

a. Write on the board: **ever, other, her, never.**
b. Point to **ever.** Everybody, read this word the fast way. Get ready. (Signal.) *Ever.* Yes, **ever.**
c. Everybody, say the sounds you write for the word (pause) **ever.** Get ready. Touch **e, v, er** as the children say *eee* (pause) *vvv* (pause) *er.* Repeat until firm.
d. Erase **ever.** Everybody, write the word (pause) **ever.** Check work.
e. Repeat *b* through *d* for **other, her,** and **never.**

TASK 3 Say the sounds, write **thing, got, wish, where**

a. You're going to write the word (pause) **thing.** Say the sounds in **thing.** Get ready. Clap for each sound as the children say *th* (pause) *ing.* Repeat until firm.
b. Everybody, write the word (pause) **thing.** Check work.
c. Repeat *a* and *b* for **got, wish,** and **where.**

TASK 4 Write **shot, salt, went, get, is**

a. You're going to write the word (pause) **shot.** Think about the sounds in **shot** and write the word. Check work.
b. Repeat *a* for **salt, went, get,** and **is.**

SENTENCE WRITING

TASK 5   Write two sentences

a. Listen to this sentence.
He has a nut and a cat.
Say that sentence. Get ready. (Signal.)
He has a nut and a cat.
b. Now you're going to say that sentence the slow way. Get ready. (Signal.) Signal for each word as the children say, *He* (pause) *has* (pause) *a* (pause) *nut* (pause) *and* (pause) *a* (pause) *cat.*
c. Everybody, write the sentence. Spell each word the right way. Check work.
d. Repeat *a* through *c* for **We are on a farm.**

LESSON 71

SOUND WRITING

TASK 1   Write **wh, er, al**

a. Everybody, you're going to write the letters that go together and make the sound **wh**. What sound? (Signal.) *wh.*
b. Write **wh**. Check work.
c. Repeat *a* and *b* for **er** and **al**.

WORD WRITING

TASK 2   Say the sounds, write **other, card, leg, beg**

a. You're going to write the word (pause) **other**. Say the sounds in **other**. Get ready. Clap for each sound as the children say *ooo* (pause) *th* (pause) *er*. Repeat until firm.
b. Everybody, write the word (pause) **other**. Check work.
c. Repeat *a* and *b* for **card, leg,** and **beg.**

TASK 3   Write **her, what, up, where, come, with, also**

a. You're going to write the word (pause) **her**. Think about the sounds in **her** and write the word. Check work.
b. Repeat *a* for **what, up, where, come, with,** and **also.**

SENTENCE WRITING

TASK 4   Write two sentences

a. Listen to this sentence.
She has a hat and a rat.
Say that sentence. Get ready. (Signal.)
She has a hat and a rat.
b. Now you're going to say that sentence the slow way. Get ready. (Signal.) Signal for each word as the children say, *She* (pause) *has* (pause) *a* (pause) *hat* (pause) *and* (pause) *a* (pause) *rat.*
c. Everybody, write the sentence. Spell each word the right way. Check work.
d. Repeat *a* through *c* for **We are on the ship.**

LESSON 72

SOUND WRITING

TASK 1   Write **wh, al, er**

a. Everybody, you're going to write the letters that go together and make the sound **wh**. What sound? (Signal.) *wh.*
b. Write **wh**. Check work.
c. Repeat *a* and *b* for **al** and **er.**

WORD WRITING

TASK 2   Say the sounds, write **ring, leg, said, other, brother**

a. You're going to write the word (pause) **ring**. Say the sounds in **ring**. Get ready. Clap for each sound as the children say *rrr* (pause) *ing*. Repeat until firm.
b. Everybody, write the word (pause) **ring**. Check work.
c. Repeat *a* and *b* for **leg, said, other,** and **brother.**

TASK 3   Write **when, what, shot, met, got, them**

a. You're going to write the word (pause) **when**. Think about the sounds in **when** and write the word. Check work.
b. Repeat *a* for **what, shot, met, got,** and **them.**

SENTENCE WRITING

TASK 4   Write three sentences

a. Listen to this sentence.
   That bus will not stop.
   Say that sentence. Get ready.   (Signal.)
   That bus will not stop.
b. Now you're going to say that sentence the
   slow way. Get ready.   (Signal.) Signal for
   each word as the children say, *That* (pause)
   bus (pause) *will* (pause) *not* (pause) *stop.*
c. Everybody, write the sentence. Spell each
   word the right way.   Check work.
d. Repeat *a* through *c* for **The men are sad**
   and **She has a dog.**

LESSON 73

SOUND WRITING

TASK 1   Write al, wh, er

a. Everybody, you're going to write the letters
   that go together and make the sound **all**.
   What sound?   (Signal.) *All.*
b. Write **all**.   Check work.
c. Repeat *a* and *b* for **wh** and **er**.

WORD WRITING

**TASK 2   Say the sounds, write rug, bug,
brother, ever**

a. You're going to write the word   (pause)
   rug. Say the sounds in **rug**. Get ready.
   Clap for each sound as the children say
   rrr (pause) *uuu* (pause) *g*. Repeat until firm.
b. Everybody, write the word   (pause) **rug**.
   Check work.
c. Repeat *a* and *b* for **bug, brother,** and **ever**.

**TASK 3   Write where, shot, beg, top, cop,
other**

a. You're going to write the word   (pause)
   where. Think about the sounds in **where**
   and write the word.   Check work.
b. Repeat *a* for **shot, beg, top, cop,** and
   other.

SENTENCE WRITING

TASK 4   Write three sentences

a. Listen to this sentence.
   His car will not run.
   Say that sentence. Get ready.   (Signal.)
   His car will not run.
b. Now you're going to say that sentence the
   slow way. Get ready.   (Signal.) Signal for
   each word as the children say, *His* (pause)
   car (pause) *will* (pause) *not* (pause) *run.*
c. Everybody, write the sentence. Spell each
   word the right way.   Check work.
d. Repeat *a* through *c* for **She did not fall** and
   Her dog is fat.

LESSON 74

WORD WRITING

**TASK 1   Say the sounds, write never, after,
also, other, mother**

a. You're going to write the word   (pause)
   never. Say the sounds in **never**. Get
   ready.   Clap for each sound as the children
   say *nnn* (pause) *eee* (pause) *vvv* (pause) *er*.
   Repeat until firm.
b. Everybody, write the word   (pause) **never**.
   Check work.
c. Repeat *a* and *b* for **after, also, other,** and
   mother.

**TASK 2   Write to, what, arm, when,
brother, had**

a. You're going to write the word   (pause) **to**.
   Think about the sounds in **to** and write the
   word.   Check work.
b. Repeat *a* for **what, arm, when, brother, had**.

SENTENCE WRITING

TASK 3   Write three sentences

a. Listen to this sentence.
   That cop can sing.
   Say that sentence. Get ready.   (Signal.)
   That cop can sing.
b. Now you're going to say that sentence the
   slow way. Get ready.   (Signal.) Signal for
   each word as the children say, *That* (pause)
   cop (pause) *can* (pause) *sing.*
c. Everybody, write the sentence. Spell each
   word the right way.   Check work.
d. Repeat *a* through *c* for **He did not hit her**
   and **She has a fish.**

LESSON 75

WORD WRITING

TASK 1   Say the sounds, write **are, mother**

a. You're going to write the word (pause) **are**. Say the sounds in **are**. Get ready. Clap for each sound as the children say *ar* (pause) *ēēē*. Repeat until firm.
b. Everybody, write the word (pause) **are**. Check work.
c. Repeat *a* and *b* for **mother**.

TASK 2   Write **him, with, went, fun, got, after, tall, cow**

a. You're going to write the word (pause) **him**. Think about the sounds in **him** and write the word.   Check work.
b. Repeat *a* for **with, went, fun, got, after, tall,** and **cow**.

SENTENCE WRITING

TASK 3   Write three sentences

a. Listen to this sentence. **We will never run.** Say that sentence. Get ready.   (Signal.) *We will never run.*
b. Now you're going to say that sentence the slow way. Get ready.   (Signal.) Signal for each word as the children say, *We* (pause) *will* (pause) *never* (pause) *run.*
c. Everybody, write the sentence. Spell each word the right way.   Check work.
d. Repeat *a* through *c* for **He can hop and sing** and **We are on the ship.**

LESSON 76

WORD WRITING

TASK 1   Say the sounds, write **her, win, said, where, has**

a. You're going to write the word (pause) **her**. Say the sounds in **her**. Get ready. Clap for each sound as the children say *h* (pause) *er*. Repeat until firm.
b. Everybody, write the word (pause) **her**. Check work.
c. Repeat *a* and *b* for **win, said, where,** and **has.**

TASK 2   Write **bark, stop, ever, sing, of, dish**

a. You're going to write the word (pause) **bark**. Think about the sounds in **bark** and write the word.   Check work.
b. Repeat *a* for **stop, ever, sing, of,** and **dish.**

SENTENCE WRITING

TASK 3   Write three sentences

a. Listen to this sentence. **That man went with him.** Say that sentence. Get ready.   (Signal.) *That man went with him.*
b. Now you're going to say that sentence the slow way. Get ready.   (Signal.) Signal for each word as the children say, *That* (pause) *man* (pause) *went* (pause) *with* (pause) *him.*
c. Everybody, write the sentence. Spell each word the right way.   Check work.
d. Repeat *a* through *c* for **The men are in the barn** and **He has a ball.**

LESSON 77

SOUND WRITING

TASK 1   Introduce sound combination **ck**

a. Write on the board: **ck**.
b. Point to **ck**. Everybody, tell me the sound these letters make. Get ready.   (Signal.) *k.* Yes, **k**.
c. Erase **ck**. Everybody, write the letters that go together and make the sound **k**. Check work.

WORD WRITING

TASK 2   Say the sounds, write **hand, when, ship**

a. You're going to write the word (pause) **hand**. Say the sounds in **hand**. Get ready. Clap for each sound as the children say *h* (pause) *aaa* (pause) *nnn* (pause) *d.* Repeat until firm.
b. Everybody, write the word (pause) **hand**. Check work.
c. Repeat *a* and *b* for **when** and **ship.**

TASK 3   Write **top, hop, cop, swim, other, brother, card, if**

a. You're going to write the word (pause) **top**. Think about the sounds in **top** and write the word.   Check work.
b. Repeat *a* for **hop, cop, swim, other, brother, card,** and **if.**

SENTENCE WRITING

TASK 4　Write three sentences

a. Listen to this sentence.
That ham is on the dish.
Say that sentence. Get ready.　(Signal.)
That ham is on the dish.
b. Now you're going to say that sentence the slow way. Get ready.　(Signal.) Signal for each word as the children say, *That* (pause) *ham* (pause) *is* (pause) *on* (pause) *the* (pause) *dish.*
c. Everybody, write the sentence. Spell each word the right way.　Check work.
d. Repeat *a* through *c* for **This dog can dig** and **She went with him.**

LESSON 78

SOUND WRITING

TASK 1　Introduce sound combination ck

a. Write on the board: **ck.**
b. Point to **ck.** Everybody, tell me the sound these letters make. Get ready.　(Signal.) *k.* Yes, **k.**
c. Erase **ck.** Everybody, write the letters that go together and make the sound **k.**　Check work.

WORD WRITING

TASK 2　Write sound combination words rock, sock, sack, pick

a. Write on the board: **rock, sock, sack,** and **pick.**
b. Point to **rock.** Everybody, read this word the fast way. Get ready.　(Signal.) *Rock.* Yes, **rock.**
c. Everybody, say the sounds you write for the word　(pause) **rock.** Get ready.　Touch **r, o, ck** as the children say *rrr* (pause) *ooo* (pause) *k.* Repeat until firm.
d. Erase **rock.** Everybody, write the word (pause) **rock.**　Check work.
e. Repeat *b* through *d* for **sock, sack,** and **pick.**

TASK 3　Say the sounds, write how, bark, where

a. You're going to write the word (pause) **how.** Say the sounds in **how.** Get ready. Clap for each sound as the children say *h* (pause) *ooo* (pause) *www.* Repeat until firm.
b. Everybody, write the word　(pause) **how.** Check work.
c. Repeat *a* and *b* for **bark** and **where.**

TASK 4　Write brother, mother, wall, call

a. You're going to write the word (pause) **brother.** Think about the sounds in **brother** and write the word.　Check work.
b. Repeat *a* for **mother, wall,** and **call.**

SENTENCE WRITING

TASK 5　Write two sentences

a. Listen to this sentence.
A hen can not bark.
Say that sentence. Get ready.　(Signal.)
A hen can not bark.
b. Now you're going to say that sentence the slow way. Get ready.　(Signal.) Signal for each word as the children say, *A* (pause) *hen* (pause) *can* (pause) *not* (pause) *bark.*
c. Everybody, write the sentence. Spell each word the right way.　Check work.
d. Repeat *a* through *c* for **He went with her.**

LESSON 79

SOUND WRITING

TASK 1　Write ck

a. Everybody, you're going to write the letters that go together and make the sound **k.** What sound?　(Signal.) *k.*
b. Write **k.** Check work.

WORD WRITING

TASK 2   Write sound combination words
pack, **back**, **rock**, **sock**

a. Write on the board: **pack, back, rock, sock.**
b. Point to **pack.** Everybody, read this word the fast way. Get ready.   (Signal.) *Pack.* Yes, **pack.**
c. Everybody, say the sounds you write for the word   (pause) **pack.** Get ready. Touch **p, a, ck** as the children say *p* (pause) *aaa* (pause) *k.* Repeat until firm.
d. Erase **pack.** Everybody, write the word (pause) **pack.**   Check work.
e. Repeat *b* through *d* for **back, rock,** and **sock.**

TASK 3   Say the sounds, write **with, cup, went, bag**

a. You're going to write the word   (pause) **with.** Say the sounds in **with.** Get ready. Clap for each sound as the children say *www* (pause) *iii* (pause) *th.* Repeat until firm.
b. Everybody, write the word   (pause) **with.** Check work.
c. Repeat *a* and *b* for **cup, went,** and **bag.**

TASK 4   Write **salt, bet, met, after**

a. You're going to write the word   (pause) **salt.** Think about the sounds in **salt** and write the word. Check work.
b. Repeat *a* for **bet, met,** and **after.**

SENTENCE WRITING

TASK 5   Write two sentences

a. Listen to this sentence.
   Her dog has a red ball.
   Say that sentence. Get ready.   (Signal.) *Her dog has a red ball.*
b. Now you're going to say that sentence the slow way. Get ready.   (Signal.) Signal for each word as the children say, *Her* (pause) *dog* (pause) *has* (pause) *a* (pause) *red* (pause) *ball.*
c. Everybody, write the sentence. Spell each word the right way. Check work.
d. Repeat *a* and *b* for **The other hat is big.**

END OF SPELLING LESSON 79

Note: At lesson 83 in the reading program, the children are introduced to all the letter names and begin the transition from spelling by sounds to spelling by letter names. By lesson 85, they are ready to begin a traditional spelling program. The authors recommend *Spelling Mastery*, Level A.